Teaching Maths to Pupils with Different Learning Styles

Tandi Clausen-May

Dr Tandi Clausen-May is a Principal Researcher at the National Foundation for Educational Research. She is responsible for the development of curriculum and assessment materials for use in primary and secondary schools, and has a particular interest in the mathematics education of all pupils within a mainstream setting.

Teaching Maths to Pupils with Different Learning Styles

Tandi Clausen-May

Paul Chapman Publishing

First published 2005
Reprinted 2006

Paul Chapman Publishing
A SAGE Publications Company
1 Oliver's Yard
55 City Road
London EC1Y 1SP

SAGE Publications Inc.
2455 Teller Road
Thousand Oaks, California 91320

SAGE Publications India Pvt Ltd
B-42, Panchsheel Enclave
Post Box 4109
New Delhi 110 017

Library of Congress Control Number: 2005906412

A catalogue record for this book is available from the British Library

ISBN-10: 1-4129--0358-0   ISBN-13: 978-1-4129-0358-5
ISBN-10: 1-4129-0359-9 (pbk)   ISBN-13: 978-1-4129-0359-2 (pbk)

Typeset by Pantek Arts Ltd, Maidstone, Kent
Printed on paper made from sustainable resources
Printed in Great Britain by The Cromwell Press, Trowbridge, Wiltshire

CONTENTS

The words or the language, as they are written or spoken, do not seem to play any role in my mechanism of thought. The psychical entities which seem to serve as elements in thought are certain signs and more or less clear images which can be "voluntarily" reproduced or combined … . The above-mentioned elements are, in my case, of visual and some of muscular type. Conventional words or other signs have to be sought for laboriously only in a secondary stage.

Albert Einstein, 1954: *Ideas and Opinions*. Crown Publishers. Pg 25

ACKNOWLEDGEMENTS

My sincere thanks go to my husband John, my sister Barbary and my colleague Adrian Woodthorpe, who read and re-read the drafts of this book, commenting and encouraging as they went. Also to John, Toby, Charlie, John-Martin and Jess, for all the photographs. And finally to my editor, Jude Bowen, for making it all happen.

CHAPTER 1

Introduction

■ *This book is about teaching mathematics to pupils who have learning differences, not learning difficulties.*

■ *Pupils with visual and kinaesthetic learning styles often struggle with a school curriculum that is largely based on print.*

■ *The development of 'pictures in the mind' can help all pupils to understand key mathematical concepts.*

a) Different Learning Styles in the Classroom – a Vicious Circle

This is a book about teaching maths to pupils with learning *differences*, not learning *difficulties*. Teaching and learning in our schools is, and always has been, print based. Literacy is all. Other ways of thinking – visual, kinaesthetic, practical – are discounted in the classroom. To become teachers, students must jump over a long series of hurdles, formal and informal, at school, at college and at university. These hurdles consist of print-based activities and assessments that demand a high level of linguistic and symbolic thought but take little account of other ways of thinking and learning. As a result, teachers are rarely selected for their visual or kinaesthetic abilities as these have little impact on their academic achievement. It is their verbal and numerical skills that have opened the doors to success, not their spatial skills. This may make it difficult for teachers to recognise spatial ability in their pupils, so real strengths and aptitudes are neglected as pupils are forced to struggle with a curriculum which is largely presented through printed materials that they find hard to access.

Because the curriculum is so heavily print based, 'proper' school maths is defined as maths that can be printed in a book, and preferably in text. Definitions and proofs that depend on models or dynamic geometry rather than on symbols are second best. So, for example,

The number seven is not ![hands showing seven fingers] or ●●●●● ●● , it is the symbol *7*

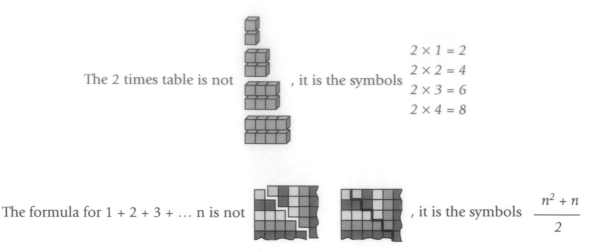

The 2 times table is not [blocks], it is the symbols

$$2 \times 1 = 2$$
$$2 \times 2 = 4$$
$$2 \times 3 = 6$$
$$2 \times 4 = 8$$

The formula for $1 + 2 + 3 + \ldots n$ is not [grids], it is the symbols $\dfrac{n^2 + n}{2}$

Pictures and models may be used to support learning, especially in the early stages, but the end point is symbolic. Symbols are easier to print, and they always take precedence over visual or kinaesthetic representations.

But to some children, the numbers and symbols on the page are just squiggles. They can *see* that seven is five plus two, or that twice two two's will fit together to make four two's, or that the sum of the first *n* counting numbers is half the area of a rectangle with sides *n* and *n* + 1. They may not be able to put it into words, but they can see it, and perhaps draw it. It is for these children, and for their teachers, that this book is written.

b) Visual, Auditory, Kinaesthetic

So – what are these different learning styles? There are nearly as many theories about learning as there are researchers writing about it. Steve Chinn offers a useful summary of 'thinking styles in mathematics', and shows how, to some extent at least, the different models overlap and inter-relate (Chinn, 2004, pp59–75). But for general classroom use the VAK model – Visual, Auditory, Kinaesthetic – will serve us well. It is at least as old as Confucius –

I hear, and I forget;

I see, and I remember;

I do, and I understand.

This model is quite straightforward, and it works well in the classroom so it can provide the theoretical structure we need for the ideas and activities discussed in this book.

The phrase *kinaesthetic learning* is sometimes taken to mean any activity that involves the use of apparatus. This may be considered particularly appropriate for 'slow learners' – at least they will have something to *do* in their mathematics lessons. But if the focus of the teaching is primarily on the correct use of the apparatus, rather than on the mathematical understanding that the apparatus is designed to develop, then it may have only a limited impact. Pupils will just follow the instructions to use the equipment, without necessarily relating what they are doing to mathematics.

Kinaesthetic learning calls for a lot more than a pile of cubes or a pair of scissors and some card. It involves using your whole being, engaging all your senses to feel or imagine what is happening. Visual, aural and kinaesthetic learning are all intertwined: together they can lay down a memory – of movement, feeling, sight and sound – that will be recalled as a total experience, not just as a recited chant. For example, when I think about the number seven I can *feel* the seven in all the fingers of one hand and two fingers of the other. When I factorise, I can imagine pulling apart *eight* to make two sets of *two twos*. And I can feel myself breaking up a 10 by 11 unit rectangle into two halves to find the sum of the first ten counting numbers, 1 + 2 + 3 + ... + 10. Because I have done all these activities, and have understood the mathematics that they represent, I do not need to actually hold up my fingers or make blocks of cubes in order to recall them. But what I recall is most certainly not a chant or a formula: it is more like a moving picture – a sort of waking dream. This, I believe, is kinaesthetic learning.

Any teaching idea, no matter how inspirational, can be reduced to 'rote learning' – *I hear and I forget*. On the other hand, the dreariest exercise might be transformed into a basis for real understanding by a teacher who can unpack the underlying concepts and help pupils to understand and use them. We all use a range of learning styles at different times, and the most effective mathematical thinkers are flexible. They try different approaches to the problem in hand, finding out what works best and relating each new idea to what they already know. The *hearing*, the *seeing* and the *doing* support one another, as the pictures, models and activities give meaning to the spoken or written definitions and procedures. Pupils may adopt different styles as they first explore and understand, and then rehearse and apply, each new concept. But for learners who think more easily in pictures and movement than in words and symbols, *seeing* and *doing* may offer access to key mathematical ideas, while too much time spent *hearing* may slam the door shut.

c) Pictures in the Mind

Some people can follow a set of directions easily, but others find it much more helpful to have a visual image. For example, one person might find it easy to follow a written description of a route:

> *Turn left out of the gate, and walk to the T-junction at the end of the road. There you should cross the road and turn right. Take the first left turn, and walk past the school and across the crossroads. You will come to another crossroads, with a church on the corner; there you must turn left. Walk about fifty metres down the road, and the house you want, number 33, is on the right, opposite the post office.*

But another might prefer a map. They find the map easier than the linear series of instructions to understand and to follow, and they can recall it more easily when they need to find their way again along the same route.

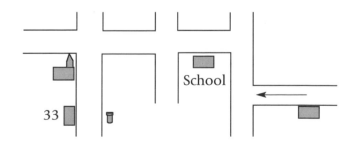

In the mathematics classroom diagrams may be used, but, as we have seen, they are generally subservient to the written, symbolic forms. A map (or its equivalent) is rarely considered to be enough on its own – while a written formula, or a set of rules for carrying out a procedure, can stand alone. Pupils who can take in and remember a series of instructions, or a formula, or the 'rules' for adding fractions or finding the sine of an angle, achieve high grades and feel successful. But those pupils for whom such rules and procedures seem meaningless have great difficulty recalling them, and cannot use them efficiently to solve problems. They may struggle to make sense of the symbols and instructions – or they may just give up in despair. Either way, they do not achieve any real understanding of the concepts that underlie the routines and methods that they are trained to use.

The main purpose of any model or image is to develop the pupils' understanding, so they do not just learn *how* to use a method to solve a problem, but they also understand *why* it works. For example, the image of a number line may help some pupils to see a subtraction as finding the 'distance' between two numbers.

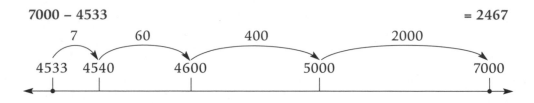

This approach may make much better sense than a standard algorithm –

7 0 0 0	6 9 9
4 5 3 3	7 0 0 0
	4 5 3 3
	2 4 6 7

Nought take away three, I can't, borrow one, I can't, borrow one, I can't, borrow one, cross out the seven and put six, make ten in the next column, cross out the ten and make nine, make ten in the next column, cross out the ten and make nine … and so on.

The number line offers far more than this sequential set of 'rules' for getting the right answer. The picture itself – whether printed, drawn, or just imagined – carries within it an explanation of why the method works. In this way, mathematical ideas from the simplest to the most complex can be made manifest, and so become meaningful and memorable to all our pupils – not just to the visual and kinaesthetic learners.

But the number line, like any other model, could be used as just another routine, to be learnt by rote and followed blindly without any understanding of the meaning of each step. Used like this it will be no more helpful, and it will be considerably less tidy, than a numerical algorithm. This book offers a range of models and images that may be useful, particularly for pupils who think more easily in pictures than in words and symbols. By themselves, however, learnt as yet more methods and routines, these models will be useless. If some pupils can, and if they really must, learn and recall mathematics without understanding, then they will do better to acquire the numerical and symbolic routines. These are generally shorter, neater, and easier to memorise and apply than the pictures and models exemplified in this book. For visual and kinaesthetic thinkers, however, this is not an option. They must understand the mathematics that they are taught. Otherwise they may learn … but they will forget.

d) Using Symbols and Understanding Diagrams

Our single most important function as maths teachers is to develop our pupils' understanding of mathematics. Using mathematical language, manipulating numbers and symbols, applying mathematics to solve problems – all this comes into it, of course. But the basis, the rock on which mathematics education is built, is understanding.

Unfortunately, it is terribly easy to teach pupils how to manipulate symbols without understanding. Any teacher with a little determination can teach *how* to add fractions, or *how* to find the area of a circle, or whatever. Pupils can learn to get 'right answers' using symbols and the rules for combining them with little understanding of what they mean. Those who can manipulate symbols quickly and efficiently are often thought to be working at a 'higher level' than those who use diagrams or equipment to work through a problem, making sense of each step on the way. As Keith Devlin puts it, 'Learn how to perform the mumbo-jumbo and you get an A' (Devlin, 2000, p67). A pupil who writes

$$\frac{2}{3} + \frac{1}{2} = \frac{2}{3} \times 2 + \frac{1}{2} \times 3 = \frac{4}{6} + \frac{3}{6} = \frac{7}{6} = 1\frac{1}{6}$$

may be rated much more highly that one who uses a more meaningful graphical approach,

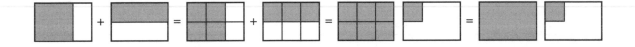

But a pupil who just goes through the steps, and cannot explain *why* $2/3$ is equal to $4/6$, and $4/6 + 3/6$ is equal to $7/6$ which is equal to $1^1/_6$, is not working at a higher level than a pupil who can use, understand and explain the drawings. The diagrams lead, not just to the 'right answer', but to an explanation – a sort of proof that $2/3 + 1/2$ really does equal $1^1/_6$. This involves much more mathematics than any rote learning of meaningless symbolic manipulation. Written numbers and symbols are valuable, and indeed essential, tools for mathematics, but we must always ensure that they are used to express, support and communicate mathematical understanding, not to take its place.

e) Identifying Different Learning Styles

All the pupils in a mathematics classroom – like all the teachers – are able to think visually and kinaesthetically to a greater or lesser degree. There is not a clear-cut divide between spatial thinkers and those who think in words and symbols. The chief difference lies, not in the ability of different pupils to think spatially or numerically, but on the value that is placed on the different thinking styles. But how can teachers spot visual and kinaesthetic ability, and identify pupils who are likely to learn more effectively through models that they can construct and take apart, and through 'pictures in the mind'?

Teachers may well notice the visual and kinaesthetic thinkers in their classroom by their responses to different types of mathematical task. These are the pupils who have found all the nets of a cube before most of the rest of the class have grasped what a net is – but for whom 'seven eights' are 'forty-three' on Tuesday, and 'sixty-two' on Wednesday. With a print-based curriculum they rarely shine – but just occasionally they take everyone (including, quite possibly, themselves) by surprise with their ability to just see the solution to a problem with which other pupils are struggling.

There are more formal approaches to the identification of pupils with high spatial ability. Many schools in the UK routinely screen pupils with the NFER-Nelson (2001) *Cognitive Ability Tests*. These give three different scores for each pupil: a Verbal Reasoning score, a Quantitative Reasoning score, and a Non-verbal Reasoning score (Strand, 2003, p5). A pupil with high spatial but low symbolic and numerical ability will be likely to have a high Non-verbal Reasoning but a lower Verbal Reasoning score. As Steve Strand explains in his book, *Getting the Best from CAT*, such pupils may have difficulty accessing much of the school curriculum. On the other hand, pupils with high Verbal Reasoning scores

> *tend to have higher national test and examination attainment than pupils with a similar mean CAT score who have their strength on the Quantitative or Non-verbal batteries.*
> *(Strand, 2003, p41)*

He argues that

> *Verbal ability is so crucial to academic success that interventions to directly address … verbal weaknesses may be necessary, especially where verbal scores are low.*
> *(Strand, 2003, p49)*

On the other hand,

> *a relative verbal strength can compensate for lower scores in the quantitative and non-verbal areas.*
> *(Strand, 2003, p42)*

This evidence again indicates the importance given to verbal ability in our educational system. High verbal ability can compensate for a lack of other sorts of learning ability – but other strengths, such as high spatial ability, cannot. Spatial ability is undervalued, and is not usually exploited to compensate for a lack of verbal ability in enabling pupils to access the curriculum.

Another more specialised series of Spatial Reasoning Tests is also available (Smith and Lord, 2002). These give teachers the means to routinely identify pupils with strong spatial ability, and so, with time, may encourage the development of a range of approaches which build more effectively on their strengths.

f) Assessment for Learning

Assessment drives the curriculum. This is regrettable, certainly. It would be much better if a broad and balanced curriculum could be established and taught, with assessment following, not leading, the whole process. But the reality is otherwise. If a topic or a mathematical idea is never assessed, then in many cases at least it will not be learnt.

Formal written maths tests tend to militate against teaching for understanding, because it is so hard to write a markable test question that actually does assess the *why* rather than the *how* (Clausen-May, 2001, p8). As Black and Wiliam argue in their booklet, *Inside the Black Box*,

> short external tests ... can dominate teachers' work, and insofar as they encourage drilling to produce right answers to short out-of-context questions, this dominance can draw teachers away from the paths to effective formative work.
> (Black and Wiliam, 1998, p17)

'Effective formative work' focuses on pupils' understanding – on finding what they understand now, and building on this to develop their understanding in the future. It is best done informally, in the everyday interchange between teachers and pupils. And since formative assessment focuses on the pupils' understanding, on the *why* rather than the *how*, it supports the use of a full range of teaching and learning styles.

Assessment for learning enables teachers to relate what pupils are learning now to what they have learnt in the past, and to pave the way for what they will learn in the future. The aim is to help pupils at all stages of mathematical development to recognise the links between the different aspects of mathematics and the various individual topics that they meet. An often quoted example is in the connections between decimals, fractions and percentages (Askew et al., 1997, p 26). Pupils learn to 'convert' from one to another, and hopefully to understand the relationships between them.

For visual and kinaesthetic thinkers, however, mathematics is shot through with connections. Multiplication may be seen and understood as area. Fractions, fractions of a turn, angle and telling the time may all be tied together through the image of a clock face. Ratio and place value may be thought of as concepts relating primarily to mathematical similarity – to shapes and solids that expand and contract without distorting. And so on. So for a visual and kinaesthetic thinker the distinctions between Number, Algebra, Shape, Space and Measures, and Data Handling may be very blurred. But are these, in any case, strictly mathematical distinctions? They are useful administrative and organisational categories, and they lie at the heart of the school mathematics curriculum. But they do not, perhaps, lie at the heart of mathematics.

This book is written to help teachers to recognise those pupils who think more easily in pictures and movement than in words and symbols, and to help them to find or build the visual and kinaesthetic 'pictures in the mind' that they need. There is not just one model that will work for every topic for every pupil – there are many possibilities. The chapters that follow offer a range of suggestions, relating to a variety of topics at different levels, but teachers may well have others that work better in their classrooms. The ideas put forward here are intended primarily as illustrations of an approach – an approach that seeks out 'models to think with' that can help pupils to develop their understanding. Some of these ideas may be useful for particular pupils, but they are only a start. Teachers – and the pupils themselves – need to be constantly alert, on the lookout for images and models that will represent and explicate specific concepts. You can start with practically any resource or activity, and see how it could be adapted for visual and kinaesthetic learners. It is the approach that matters, not the details of particular activities or materials. Making mathematical concepts manifest with pictures and models will help all pupils – even those who could, if it were really demanded of them, learn and remember routines for getting 'right answers'.

Introduction – Key Points

- Children have different learning styles – Visual, Auditory and Kinaesthetic (VAK).

- The school curriculum is heavily print based. This favours auditory learners.

- Visual and kinaesthetic thinking and learning styles are under-valued in the classroom.

- Visual and kinaesthetic learners need a 'picture in the mind' to hang their thinking on.

- A visual approach is worthwhile only if it is based on understanding.

- Mathematical symbols are there to express, support and communicate understanding, not to take its place.

- Teachers can identify pupils with different learning styles informally, through observation, or more formally, using a range of tests.

- Assessment for learning supports teaching for understanding.

- Appropriate models will help pupils to recognise links between different aspects of mathematics.

CHAPTER 2

The Concept of Number

- *Pupils' understanding of Number is key to their mathematical development.*

- *Numbers may be **counted** in a sequence or **seen** as wholes.*

- *Pupils spend a lot of time counting, but less attention may be paid to seeing the whole.*

- *Kinaesthetic and visual representations of numbers will help all pupils to understand numbers as wholes.*

a) Counting and Seeing

When numbers are written on paper or shown on a calculator screen they are represented by a set of abstract symbols, which to many children are mere squiggles. Children train long and hard to learn which squiggle to associate with which sound – *1* with *one*, *2* with *two*, and so on. They recite the sounds in turn, as they learn to count a group of objects. But the outcome of all this counting and sequential recitation may be to build up an understanding of each number as a *collection of ones*, rather than as a concept in its own right. *Five*, for example, is given meaning and existence primarily as *the number that comes after four*. There is no real understanding of the fiveness of five. Rather, it is seen as the result of *one add one add one add one add one*.

But this focus on the sequential nature of numbers is not the only one possible. It has perhaps been forced on us in the school curriculum by our reliance on print, but we, as teachers, have other resources available that encourage a different approach. For some children – and particularly for visual and kinaesthetic thinkers – a more holistic approach, which emphasises the nature of each number as a whole rather than as a collection of units, may be much more meaningful.

Most people can scan up to four objects, and see at a glance how many there are, without counting (Butterworth, 1999, p304). This ability to *subitise*, as it is called, lies at the heart of the holistic approach to Number. We can see a collection of four dots, or fingers, or objects, and know that there are four, with no need to go through the sequential process of counting *one, two, three, four*. Some arrangements are easier to see than others, but we can learn to recognise the number of objects in any group of up to four.

So we can understand *four* not as *one add one add one add one*, but as an image of four objects. Similarly for *one*, *two* or *three*, we can see the whole, not just the sequence of parts.

So much for numbers up to *four*. But this is a bit limited. How can we go further?

The first and most readily available resource is literally to hand. We can learn to see (*see*, not count) up to four fingers on one hand.

But because it is a coherent whole, we can also see the whole hand, and we can learn that this is a representation of *five* – although other, more random representations of five are much harder to just 'see'. They may have to be counted.

 is easier to see (*not count*) than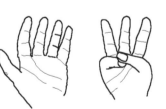

So now we have the numbers *one* to *five*, each able to be represented by the digits on one hand.

But, of course, we have two hands.

So, just as we can learn to see (*not count*) that this pattern of fingers is *three*:

so, in the same way, we can learn to see (*not count*) that this pattern is *eight*:

In this way the numbers one to ten can be represented as patterns of fingers on a pair of hands. This approach helps to establish the concept of each number as a whole, rather than as a part of a sequence. It also offers concrete, rather than symbolic, images of numbers. And finally, the representation of each number involves physical movement. So children can develop an understanding of number that is based on aural, visual and kinaesthetic images. How much more powerful than any merely symbolic representation!

In the Classroom – *See and Say*

To start with, the teacher can hold up a number of fingers, and call out the total (including, sometimes, *nought* or *zero*). The children copy the teacher.

Then the teacher calls a number up to ten and the children show this on their fingers, or the teacher shows the number and the children call it.

When they are confident, one child can take the teacher's place showing or calling numbers to which the other children respond.

Parents and carers may be encouraged to play this game with individual children for a few minutes each day after school.

But … we have only five digits on each hand. Ten altogether. How can we go beyond 'ten' without symbols? This is where the abacus – some types of abacus – comes in.

b) The Slavonic Abacus

The majority of abaci that are readily available in the UK lead naturally to a 'counting' approach to Number. There are typically five or ten rows of ten beads, with each row painted a different colour – ten red beads, then ten blue, then ten yellow, and so on. Nothing about the row of ten red beads helps us to see (*not count*) numbers up to ten. Given a row of nine identical beads to look at, for example, we have no choice but to count them to discover how many there are.

 cannot be seen *without counting*.

But there are other types of abacus, which support the *seeing* rather than the *counting* approach to number. One of these is the Slavonic abacus. These are much more common in other parts of Europe than in the UK or the USA, but they are well worth finding, or making.

The Slavonic abacus has the usual ten rows of ten beads, but these are coloured with only two, or at the most four, colours, in such a way that each row and each column is made up of five beads of one colour and five of another (Grauberg, 1998, pp18–19).

One row of beads on the Slavonic abacus allows us to represent numbers up to ten. These are shown in the same way as on a pair of hands, so work on the first row of beads follows naturally from simple finger pattern arithmetic. As with the finger patterns, the emphasis is always on *seeing* whole numbers at a glance, not on counting them one by one.

We can see (*not count*) the numbers *one* to *four* in the usual way.

But now we can also see (*not count*) *five* beads, because they are distinguished by their colour from the rest of the row.

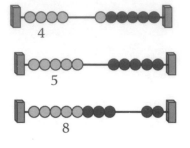

And we can learn to see (*not count*) *eight* as a pattern, with five beads of one colour and three of the other.

This approach to whole numbers up to 10 has the great strength that every number is seen with its complement to 10, so each number becomes deeply associated with its complement. The *two* that goes with *eight*, for example, becomes an inbuilt aspect of the concept of the number of *eight*.

But the way in which the beads on the Slavonic abacus are coloured allows us to go further, and to see numbers up to 100, with their complements to 100. For example, we can see that this abacus shows *seventy-two* beads – that is, seven whole rows, plus two single beads. We can also see that there are *twenty-eight* beads – two whole rows, plus eight single beads – left over to make the full complement of a hundred.

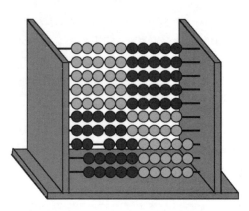

So the Slavonic abacus offers pupils a way to understand each number up to a hundred, not as a point in a recited sequence, but rather as a whole that is seen, not counted. This whole may then be associated with the relevant symbol – *6* with a row of six beads, for example, or *40* with four rows of ten. Place value and its use in the representation of multi-digit numbers is discussed in more detail in Chapter 4, but the abacus provides a visual and kinaesthetic experience which will give pupils a thorough grasp of the concept of Number. Their understanding of the symbols which are used to represent numbers will then be based on a meaningful, and therefore memorable, concept.

In the Classroom – *Numbers and their Complements*

Using a large Slavonic abacus, the teacher shows a one-digit number on the top row. The children call the number, and then they call its complement to ten. They may also show first the number, then its complement, on their fingers.

In the same way, the teacher uses the whole abacus to show a two-digit number, being careful to move all the rows of *ten* in one movement, followed by the *one* beads. So to show the number *forty-six*, for example, the teacher moves the top four rows of the abacus across, and the children call 'forty … '.

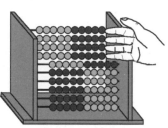

Then the teacher moves six beads in the fifth row across, and the children call ' … six'.

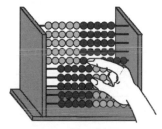

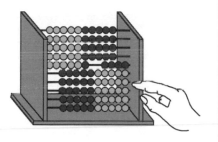

Now the teacher points to the remaining beads, and the children say, 'and fifty-four make a hundred'.

If a Slavonic abacus is unavailable then an overhead projector slide with a coloured transparent plastic sheet cut to mask dots to the right and below the number being shown, or a block of interlocking cubes, may be used instead to convey the same ideas. Pupils may use a scaled-down version of the grid, with a smaller transparent plastic sheet.

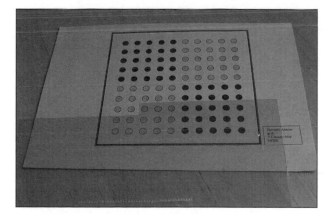

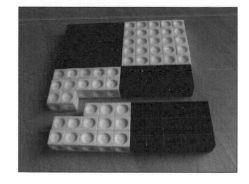

Photocopiable Resource Sheets 1 and 2 may be used to create the grids. Alternatively, teachers can download a free electronic Slavonic abacus from the Xavier website at the University of Bangor (go to www.xavier.bangor.ac.uk/xavier, and try all the options for 'Slavonic Abacus'). However, neither the static grid and model nor the electronic abacus offer the same kinaesthetic experience as an actual Slavonic abacus made of beads that can be manipulated by the teacher and the pupils. A large classroom abacus may be bought from the Xavier website, or from Class Creations (www.classcreations.co.uk).

The Concept of Number – Key Points

■ A lot of time and effort is spent teaching children to count.

■ Children who think more easily in pictures and movements (**visual** and **kinaesthetic** learners) may do better with a more holistic approach.

■ Representing whole numbers up to 10 on a pair of hands enables children to see and feel the mathematical structure of numbers.

■ One- and two-digit numbers may be represented on a Slavonic abacus.

■ Pupils can see the complements to 10 or 100 of numbers represented on the Slavonic abacus.

■ Such representations enable pupils to **see**, not count, a number of objects. This is called **subitising**.

Models for Multiplication and Division

- *Multiplication may be understood using an area model.*

- *Single-digit multiplication may be modelled on the Slavonic abacus.*

- *An image of a large rectangle divided into smaller rectangles may be used to understand long multiplication.*

- *A different 'picture in the mind', modelling the process of repeated subtraction, is needed for long division.*

a) Multiplication Arrays – 'Seeing' up to Four Fours

To visual and kinaesthetic thinkers, arithmetic can seem very daunting. There are so many numbers. Masses of those wretched squiggles, and endless rules for putting them together. To pupils who think more easily in pictures than in words and symbols neither the squiggles nor the rules will make much sense. So the challenge for the teacher is to find ways of presenting the important concepts with models, visual and kinaesthetic 'pictures in the mind', on which to hang them.

Multiplying two numbers can always be thought of as finding the area of a rectangle. Pupils can learn to recognise arrays of up to four by four, and associate them with their totals. So, for example, they can see the array ◯ ◯ ◯ / ◯ ◯ ◯ as two rows of three, and they can learn to recognise this as *six*.

Arrays like this may be printed onto cards, to be handled by pupils until they become very familiar. These cards do not have a 'right way up' – so, for example, it is clear that:

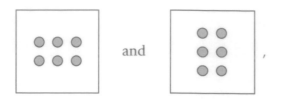 are both equally *six*. The concept of commutativity – that *two threes* are the same as *three twos* – becomes established as a fact relating to the patterns of dots, not to the inter-changeability of squiggles.

Similarly, the squareness of square numbers becomes self-evident –

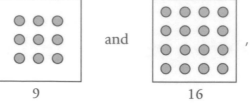

for example, are square numbers because they are square, not just because they are squiggles multiplied by themselves.

In the Classroom – *Dotty Arrays*

Photocopy masters for a set of cards showing each of the arrays from one by two to four by four may be downloaded from the Paul Chapman Publishing website, www.paulchapmanpublishing.co.uk/clausen-may. Working with the whole class, the teacher holds up each array in turn and the pupils call both the total product and its two factors. Photocopiable Resource Sheet 3 can be used to prepare sets of array cards for individual pupils. When they are confident, pupils can work in pairs to build up speed so they can instantly recognise, for example, the three by four array as *twelve* whatever its orientation – three by four, four by three, or on a slant.

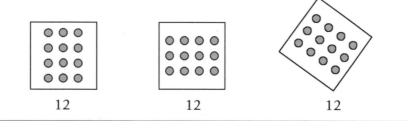

In the Classroom – *Factorising*

Blocks of interlocking cubes can also be used to represent each array. These have the advantage that they can be split up and re-combined, to demonstrate the process of factorisation – so *four threes*, for example, can be broken up and reassembled into *two sixes*.

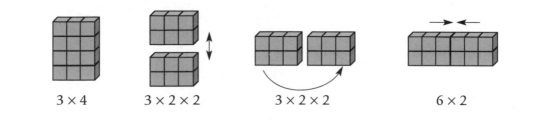

Just as pupils can learn to see, *not count*, a row or column of up to four beads, so they can learn to see, *not count*, an array up to of up to four by four beads. This will give them the 'pictures in the mind' they need to enable them to visualise, and so recall, the multiplication facts up to 4 × 4. These need to be established first, before pupils go on to work with multiplication facts involving larger numbers, 5 and above.

b) Multiplying up to Ten by Ten

Just as it is hard to see, *not count*, a row or column of seven or eight identical beads, so it is hard to see, *not count*, an array involving a pair of such numbers, such as *seven eights*. But here again, the Slavonic abacus can provide the 'picture in the mind' that we need.

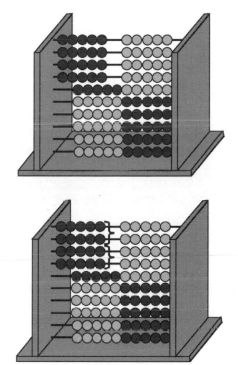

First, pupils must learn to recognise the products in the five times table. These may be modelled using the beads on one side of the Slavonic abacus. So *four fives*, for example, may be represented as four rows of five beads.

These four rows are then grouped into pairs, to give *two tens*.

Alternatively, this relationship can be modelled with interlocking cubes. The four rows of five can be broken up into two blocks of two by five, then joined up again to make two rows of ten.

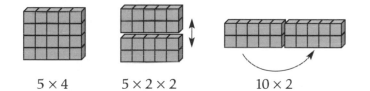

5 × 4	5 × 2 × 2	10 × 2

In the Classroom – *Multiplying by Five*

Teachers can use the Slavonic abacus to demonstrate a multiplication fact for five, such as the relationship between *seven fives* and *three tens plus five*.

Then pupils can use interlocking cubes to build a model of the same relationship, and of others in the five times table.

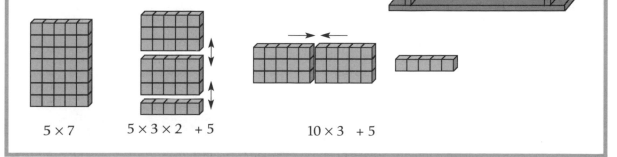

5 × 7	5 × 3 × 2 + 5	10 × 3 + 5

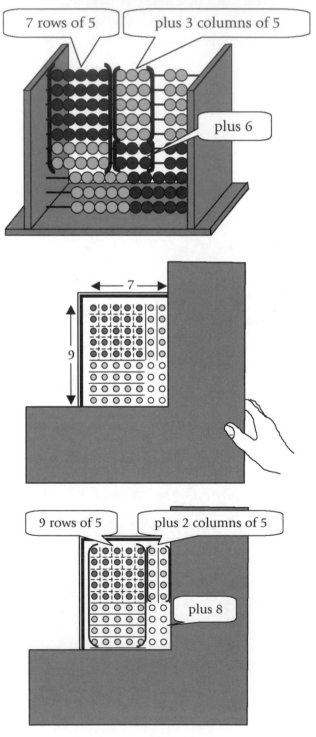

Once pupils know the products up to ten times five – and understand them as rearrangements of the fives into pairs to make tens – they can go on to multiply higher single digit numbers.

To create a model for the product of *seven* and *eight*, for example, an array of seven rows of eight must be set up on the abacus. Pupils should be able to set this array in one movement, selecting the seven rows of eight beads at a glance, without counting.

7 rows of 5   plus 3 columns of 5

plus 6

The array on the Slavonic abacus splits into four rectangles, identified by their colours. On the left are two rectangles, comprising seven rows of five – five in one colour, and two in the other. On the right are three *columns* of five in one colour, plus a three by two rectangle. So altogether we have ten fives – seven rows of five plus three columns of five – plus six, giving a total of fifty-six.

Here again a printed grid, this time with an L-shaped shield to mark off the product being calculated, may be used if no Slavonic abacus is available (see Photocopiable Resource Sheet 4). So to calculate the product of *nine* and *seven*, for example, we shield off an array of nine rows of seven.

7

9

This gives nine rows of five on the left, plus two columns of five on the right, plus eight. So we have eleven fives plus eight, or fifty-five plus eight, which is sixty-three.

9 rows of 5   plus 2 columns of 5

plus 8

In the Classroom – *Practising the Multiplication Tables*

Teachers can set up arrays on the Slavonic abacus for the products of single digits, and pupils can first say what product is being represented and then give the total. When they are confident, pupils can practise using the abacus or the grid to find products of pairs of single digits by themselves. With time, they will develop a mental image of the arrays on a Slavonic abacus, which they can recall and use to calculate the elusive number facts of the multiplication tables.

This approach to single-digit multiplication may well seem tedious and long-winded to those pupils who are able to simply learn the 'magic spells' of the multiplication tables –

> *Grue chups are glonk*

> *Grue sleps are fruggle*

and so on. But for pupils for whom the spells never come out the same way twice running, a 'picture in the mind' may be much more meaningful. For visual and kinaesthetic learners, learning without understanding is not an option – they will just forget. So in the long run, although it takes more effort to 'see' the rows and columns of five and the rectangle in the bottom right corner, and to put all the beads together to find the product, a mental image of the Slavonic abacus is much easier to recall when it is needed. But here again, if the use of the Slavonic abacus is taught as just another method, a series of steps to be followed blindly in order to find a right answer, it will not help at all. The abacus does not simply state that 'seven eights are fifty-six': it offers a visible representation of the number fifty-six as the product of seven and eight. If pupils are to remember this method, and to use it effectively, then they must understand the *why*, not just know the *how*.

c) Multi-digit Multiplication – the Area Model

The 'rules' for long multiplication are amongst the most confusing and incomprehensible that pupils have to contend with.

> *Multiply the end underneath number by each of the top numbers in turn, carrying the left-hand digit whenever the answer is more than nine. Then put a nought on the end of the next line, and multiply the next underneath number by each of the top numbers. Then if there is another underneath number you put two noughts on the next line, and … and so on. Oh – and you work the other way round from the way you read: right to left, not left to right.*

Just remembering when and where to put in the noughts is hard! Doing each of the computations in turn, in the right order, without ever losing one's place – that is well nigh impossible for many pupils.

In the Classroom – *Handy Multiplication*

Another method for finding the harder multiplication facts from the six, seven, eight and nine times tables is also worth mentioning. It involves memorising a routine – but the routine is something to do, rather than something to say, so it may be helpful for kinaesthetic learners who can remember movements more easily than words.

The thumb and fingers of each hand are first labelled with the numbers 6 to 10.

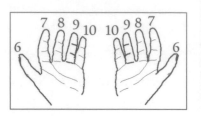

Then the tips of the two fingers whose numbers are to be multiplied are brought together so they are just touching. For example, to multiply 7 by 8 the tip of the forefinger (labelled 7) must just touch the tip of the middle finger (labelled 8) to form a link. Now the two touching fingers, and all the fingers (and the thumbs) above them, are counted, giving 2 on one hand and 3 on the other – or 5 altogether. This is the number of *tens* in the total product.

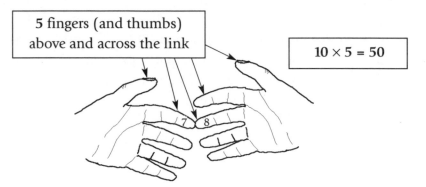

5 fingers (and thumbs) above and across the link

10 × 5 = 50

Next we look at the fingers below the link. There are 3 on one hand and 2 on the other. These two numbers are multiplied together, and the product, *6*, is added to the *5 tens* we already have.

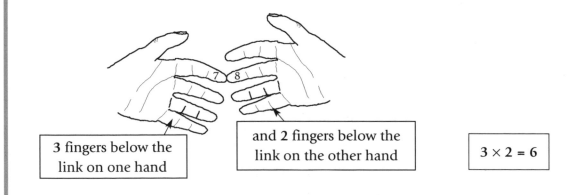

3 fingers below the link on one hand

and 2 fingers below the link on the other hand

3 × 2 = 6

So 7 times 8 is *5 tens, plus 6* – or 56 altogether.

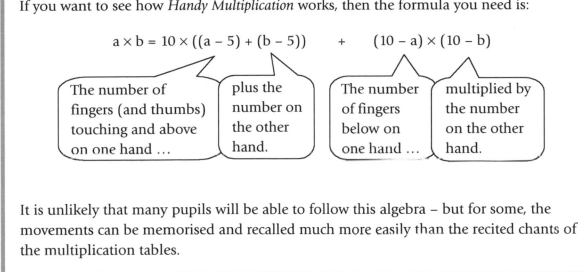

If you want to see how *Handy Multiplication* works, then the formula you need is:

$$a \times b = 10 \times ((a - 5) + (b - 5)) \qquad + \qquad (10 - a) \times (10 - b)$$

The number of fingers (and thumbs) touching and above on one hand …

plus the number on the other hand.

The number of fingers below on one hand …

multiplied by the number on the other hand.

It is unlikely that many pupils will be able to follow this algebra – but for some, the movements can be memorised and recalled much more easily than the recited chants of the multiplication tables.

Fortunately, the 'area' model for multi-digit multiplication has recently become much more common in our classrooms. The 1999 Key Stage 3 Mathematics Tests had a question in the non-calculator paper that used this approach. Pupils were first offered an area model for the calculation *18 × 14*. They were then asked to carry out exactly the same computation, but this time presented as a conventional multiplication. This might appear to be asking the same question twice – but, as the *Standards at Key Stage 3 – Mathematics* report for 1999 indicates, while 56% of the pupils taking the test found the area of the rectangle, only 49% gave the correct response to 18 × 14 (QCA, 2000).

Key Stage 3 Mathematics Test Question (1999)

This diagram shows a rectangle 18cm long and 14cm wide.

It has been split into four smaller rectangles.

Write the area of each small rectangle on the diagram.

One has been done for you.

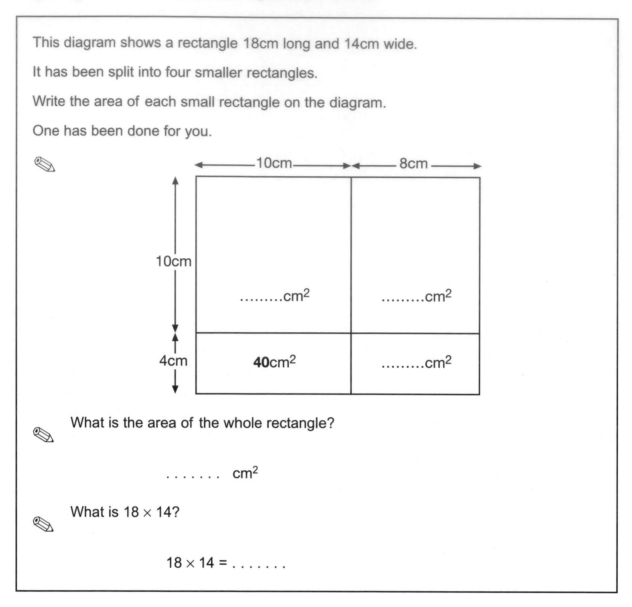

What is the area of the whole rectangle?

. . . . cm^2

What is 18 × 14?

18 × 14 = ...

Sadly, many pupils calculated the area of the rectangle correctly using the diagram given, but then started again with the computation *18 × 14* using a written algorithm. They were more likely to get this wrong, and some pupils then went back and changed their original correct answer for the area of the rectangle to their incorrect solution to the long multiplication. For example, Alison wrote:

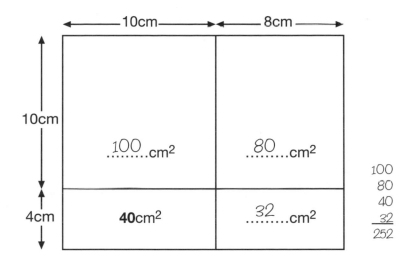

What is the area of the whole rectangle?

.....~~202~~... 738 cm²

What is 18 × 14?

18
× 14
──
18
720
──
738

18 × 14 = ...738...

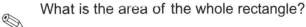

Alison's belief in the 'correct' method (that is to say, in the formal, written algorithm) in which she had been drilled undermined her confidence in the more meaningful, and therefore more reliable, area-based calculation. But, hopefully, the increased acceptance of a range of methods will, in time, encourage pupils to use the more meaningful approach even in formal test situations.

The area model of multiplication has a number of advantages over the standard written algorithm. The different parts of the computation are tied directly to different parts of the rectangle, so it is easier to keep track of them. The most significant numbers (in the example above, the '10's from the '18' and the '14') are multiplied first – while in the standard written algorithm, all the attention is focused first on the relatively insignificant 8 and 4. But above all, the area model is meaningful. It allows pupils to see *why* the '1' in the '18' multiplied by the '1' in the '14' gives '100', not '1'. Here again, to make it worthwhile pupils must understand what the model represents. Without that understanding the area model is no more memorable, and may be considerably less tidy and concise, than the conventional numerical algorithm. Checking the pupils' understanding is best done informally by the teacher in the classroom, both when long multiplication is first introduced and when it is used to solve other, more complex, problems.

d) Using the Area Model for Mental Calculation

The area model for multiplication can also offer a useful 'picture in the mind' for mental calculation. For example, finding the square of 29 using the standard written algorithm is complicated and hard to understand. It has a total of about a dozen steps – *find nine nine's; put down the one and carry the eight; find nine two's; add on the carried eight; put down the total next to the one … and so on.* All the steps must be done in exactly the right order, or the whole thing will go haywire.

But a 'picture in the mind' offers a quite different, more meaningful approach. To find the area of a square with edges 29 units long, we can start by imagining a square with edges that are 30 units long, which has an area of 900 square units.

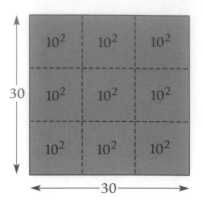

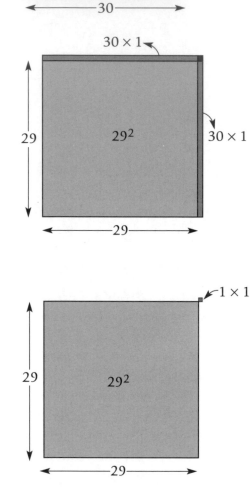

Now we strip a long thin rectangle, 30 units long and 1 unit wide, away from the top of the 30^2 square, and another one from the side. $900 - (30 + 30) = 840$

But this means that we have stripped away the single unit square in the corner twice – so we must add 1 back on to get the area of the 29^2 square. $840 + 1 = 841$

It is much easier for visual and kinaesthetic thinkers to keep track of this computation. To start with they may sketch a simple diagram, but with time they will just imagine the square with the unit-wide strips being peeled off from the top and side, and then the little 1 by 1 square that has been stripped off twice being replaced. Every step of the calculation is matched by a relevant change to the model, making it meaningful and, therefore, memorable.

These examples of the use of the area model for multiplication demonstrate the fundamental approach to making mathematics visible for visual and kinaesthetic learners. Teachers should always seek a model, sometimes physical, sometimes just a 'picture in the mind', but always an image which encapsulates the basic mathematical concepts and methods being used. The pupils then have something to hang their thinking on, so there is no need to try to remember a lot of number facts or rules for computation. The mental images speak for themselves: each step in the calculation is performed for a reason, so the whole is a meaningful operation, not a blind routine based on inevitably unreliable memory. Pupils develop strategies which enable them to work out solutions for themselves when rote memory fails – and so they become, not just 'mathematical doers', but 'mathematical thinkers'.

In the Classroom – *Stripping Edges*

Teachers can draw a series of diagrams to demonstrate the method of stripping the edges from a rectangle in order to multiply any pair of two-digit numbers.

For example, the 'picture in the mind' for 36×47 starts with a 40 by 50 rectangle.

Long thin rectangles, 50 by 4 and 40 by 3, must be stripped off the edges of the 40 by 50 rectangle.

Then a little 3 by 4 rectangle is put back in the corner where it has been taken off twice.

So:

36×47

$= (40 \times 50) - (50 \times 4) - (40 \times 3) + (4 \times 3)$

$= 2000 - 200 - 120 + 12$

$= 1692$

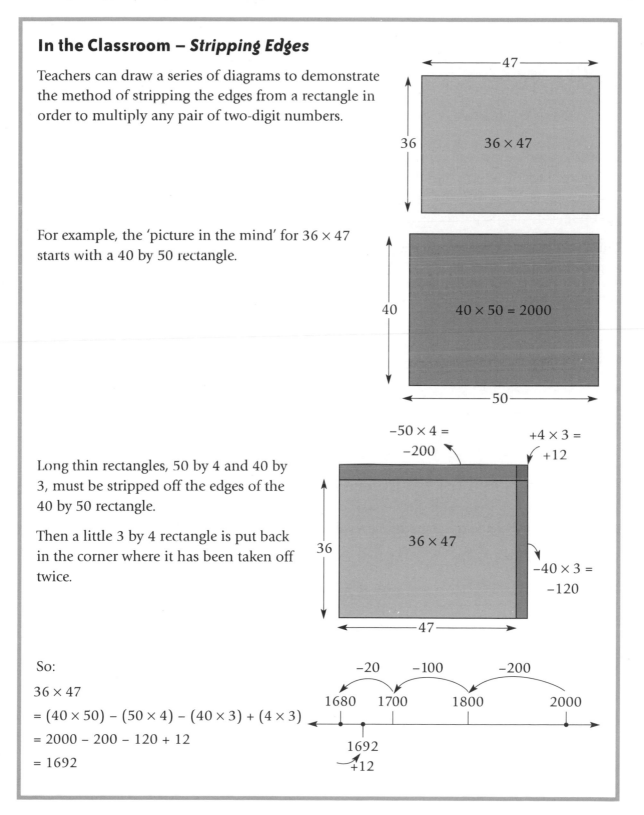

e) Division

Division is a tricky concept for all pupils – but particularly for visual and kinaesthetic thinkers. Mathematically speaking, division is the inverse of multiplication – so if *14 × 18 = 252*, for example, then *252 ÷ 14 = 18*. Using an area model for multiplication, we can say

> *The area of a 14 by 18 rectangle is 252.*

This can be re-phrased as a division to give

> *A rectangle with an area of 252 and one side of length 14 must have another side of length 18.*

The area model works well for multiplication. If I know the lengths of its two sides then I can build up a visual image of the whole rectangle. I can *imagine* the rectangle, even if I have not yet started to split it up into its smaller rectangles in order to work out its area.

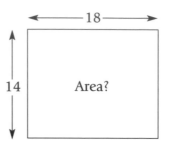

But if all I know are the area and the length of one side, it is much harder to visualise the rectangle. I do not know what shape it is.

Is it this shape?   Or this shape?   Or…. ?

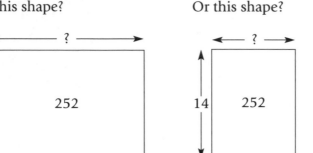

Steve Chinn recommends a 'repeated subtraction' approach to division (Chinn, 1998, p68). This does not lend itself well to the area-based image of a rectangle. Rather, it needs a more nebulous, undefined shape to represent the total product which is to be divided. A pile of counters that can be split up into a number of smaller heaps may offer a more useful 'picture in the mind' for division.

For example, 252 ÷ 14 may be thought of as 'How many 14s are there in 252?' To model this, we need a pile of 252 counters, to be sorted into heaps of 14.

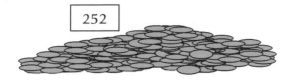

252

252 ÷ 14 = ?

Then, following Chinn's method, we subtract convenient 'chunks' from the 252, made up of easy multiples of 14. In this case we can start by taking ten heaps of 14. That is, we subtract 140 counters from our pile.

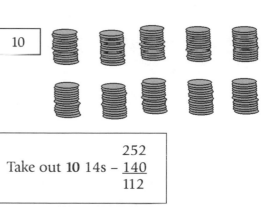

10

112

```
                    252
Take out 10 14s –  140
                    112
```

This reduces the pile considerably. We are left with 112 counters. Not enough for another ten heaps, but we can manage five more. That will remove another 70 counters from the pile.

15

42

```
                    252
Take out 10 14s  – 140
                    112
Take out 5 14s    – 70
                     42
```

Now we have fifteen heaps of 14 counters, and there are 42 left in the pile. Well, two more heaps will get rid of 28 of them.

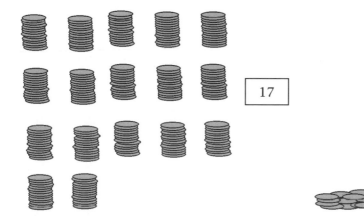

17

14

```
                    252
Take out 10 14s  – 140
                    112
Take out 5 14s    – 70
                     42
Take out 2 14s    – 28
                     14
```

That gives us seventeen heaps of 14 counters, and just 14 left in the pile. Enough for one more heap.

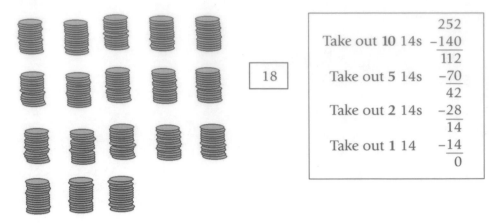

So now we have divided all our 252 counters into heaps of 14, giving us 10 + 5 + 2 + 1, or 18, heaps all together.

This example serves to illustrate Chinn's approach to division. Clearly some pupils may be able to take out larger numbers of counters in one go, while others might have to go more slowly, removing fewer counters at a time from the pile. The important point is to ensure that pupils have a 'picture in the mind' to help them to understand what is happening at each step as they divide the pile of 252 counters into heaps of 14.

Those pupils who do eventually go on to use the conventional algorithm for long division will find that the model still holds. To divide 8802 by 27, for example, we start by finding that there are **300** 27s (8100) in 8802, with 702 left. In the 702 there are **20** 27s (540), with 162 left. The remaining 162 gives us another 6 27s, so we have a total of 300 + 20 + 6, or **326** 27s in 8802.

```
        326
27 ) 8802
      8100
       702
       540
       162
       162
         0
```

Models for Multiplication and Division – Key Points

■ Arithmetic can be very daunting for visual and kinaesthetic thinkers.

■ The multiplication of two numbers is more meaningful if it is thought of as finding the area of a rectangle.

■ For single-digit multiplication, arrays and the Slavonic abacus offer useful models.

■ Long multiplication can be understood using the area method.

■ Some calculations which are hard and complicated to do using a conventional written algorithm can be done mentally using an area model.

■ Division requires a different model to multiplication.

■ The conventional algorithm for long division is based on repeated subtraction. This may be adapted using a 'picture in the mind', such as a of a pile of counters being distributed into equal-sized heaps.

CHAPTER 4

Place Value and Decimals

- *The concept of place value is essential to the representation of both whole and decimal numbers.*

- *The key to understanding place value is scale.*

- *The key to the representation of place value is movement.*

a) Whole Number Place Value

Place value in our number system tells us the size of a number. Because we use a decimal system, place value gives us the size in powers of ten – *1*s, *10*s, *100*s, *1 000*s and so on. Any number, no matter how big, is broken up into its constituent powers of ten – so *three hundred and seventy-six*, for example, is exactly what it says: three hundreds, seven tens and six ones.

The key to understanding place value is *scale*. The calculation *400 + 200*, for example, works in the same way as the calculation *4 + 2*. The numbers are similar – they are just on a bigger *scale*. *40* is ten times as much as *4*, and *400* is ten times as much as *40*, and so on. This idea lies at the heart of our representation of whole numbers. Place value is just a symbolic representation of the powers of ten, so it can be visualised as a representation of *scale*.

Place value equipment – Diennes blocks and other base 10 materials – usually represent *1* as a single unit cube, *10* as ten cubes in a stick, *100* as ten sticks in a slab and *1 000* as a ten slabs in a bigger cube.

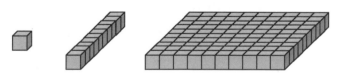
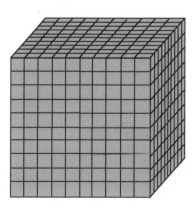

And then the cycle starts again. We can imagine, even if we cannot actually represent, ten *1 000* cubes that make up a *10 000* stick, ten *10 000* sticks in a *100 000* slab, and ten *100 000* slabs in a *1 000 000* cube. If the single unit *1* cube has an edge length of one centimetre then the *1 000* cube will be ten centimetres cubed, while the *1 000 000* cube will be a whopping metre cubed. These are much too big to make with ordinary base 10 materials, although a good model of a cubic metre may be made with twelve garden canes cut to size and fastened together at the corners. But

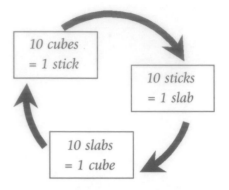

10 cubes = 1 stick

10 sticks = 1 slab

10 slabs = 1 cube

the cycle, from cubes to sticks to slabs to cubes, goes on and on. It gives us a 'picture in the mind' of whole numbers getting infinitely large, but always in a precise, controlled pattern.

It is a bit awkward, though, that the *1*, the *10* and the *100* are completely different shapes. It may be difficult to see how

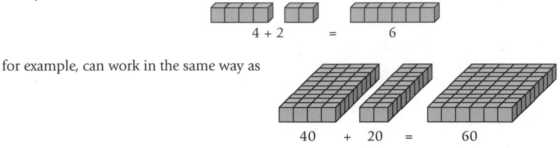

4 + 2 = 6

for example, can work in the same way as

40 + 20 = 60

The *1* cubes are there, at the ends of the *10* sticks – but the cubes and sticks are different shapes, so they cannot fit together in the same way.

On the other hand, making *1* and *10* the same shape – so they are both cubes, for instance, where the *10* cube has ten times the volume of the *1* cube – does not work either. It is not obvious that

if this is *1*: 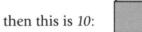 then this is *10*:

even though the *10* cube has a volume ten times greater than the *1* cube. We cannot see the ten *1*s in the *10* here, as we can see the ten *1* cubes in a *10* stick.

This being the case, children who think more easily in pictures than in words and numbers may actually find it easier to see the connection between, say, *4* and *4 000*, than between *4* and *40* or *400*. Using conventional base 10 materials, *4* is represented by four *1* cubes, and *4 000* is represented by four *1 000* cubes. The picture in the mind for *4 000 + 2 000* is exactly the same as the picture for *4 + 2* – it is just bigger.

The four *1 000* cubes are combined with the two *1 000* cubes in exactly the same way as the four *1* cubes combine with the two *1* cubes. We can see the thousand *1*s in the *1 000*, but we can also see the *1 000* as a whole, so we can think in thousands.

4 + 2 = 6

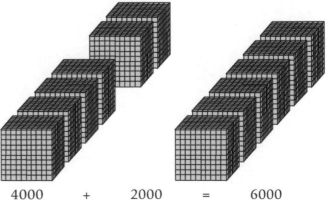

4000 + 2000 = 6000

In the Classroom – *Modelling Whole Numbers*

Pupils who have difficulty interpreting printed symbols and numerals are likely to find written work on place value hard to understand and remember. They need something, a model or a mental image, to hang the symbols on to. Teachers can use base ten equipment, or interlocking cubes such as Centicubes, to model a number with up to four digits.

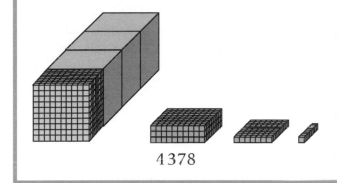

4 378

Sets of base 10 equipment rarely have more than one 1 000 cube, but it is not difficult to make these so that numbers over 2 000 can be modelled. If the 1 cube is a centimetre cube then extra 1 000 cubes, 10 centimetres by 10 centimetres by 10 centimetres, may be made from card or thick paper.

b) Decimal Place Value

The idea that *4 000* is the same shape as *4*, but bigger, suggests a way to think about decimal numbers. If *4 000* is the same as *4*, but a thousand times bigger, then *4.378*, for example, is the same as *4 378*, but a thousand times smaller. There is nothing new to learn about the numbers: we are just 'zooming in', seeing the thousand little unit cubes inside each thousand cube. The model for the two numbers is the same – but in the one case we are working with thousands, and in the other with units.

It may be useful, at this point, to make the connection with capacity. If *1* is represented by a centimetre cube, then it has a capacity of a millilitre. In that case, the *1 000* cube has a capacity of a litre. So the model can be seen as representing either 4 378 millilitres or 4.378 litres – it depends how it is viewed.

In the Classroom – *Modelling Decimal Numbers*

The same model will serve equally well to represent a 4-figure whole number, like *4 378*, or a number which is less than *10* but runs to three decimal places, such as *4.378*

In a decimal number greater than *10*, however, the centimetre cube must represent *1*, so for the decimal part of the number we need *0.1* 'slabs' on the same scale as the whole numbers. These are the slabs one would get by slicing a centimetre cube into ten. Making these may seem more difficult, but in fact thick card, from a shoe box or from the back of a pad of paper, is usually about a millimetre thick – or near enough. Centimetre squares can be cut from this card, and ten of these will lie on top of each other to form a cube (of sorts) about a centimetre high. Each of these 1 centimetre by 1 centimetre by 1 millimetre slabs represents *0.1* on the same scale as the centimetre cubes representing *1*.

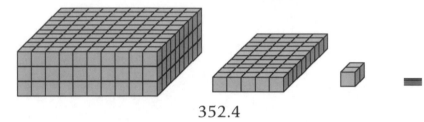

352.4

One of these card centimetre squares may again be cut into ten 'sticks' a millimetre wide, and even into millimetre cubes, to represent the *0.01*s and the *0.001*s, if these are required.

The bits of the number are getting almost too small to see and handle now – but this gets across the idea of the relative sizes of whole numbers and decimals in a very powerful manner. And while it would obviously be absurd to try to slice the tiny millimetre cubed *0.001* cube into *0.0001* slabs one tenth of a millimetre thick, the idea is there. The same cycle as we used for whole numbers, but going in reverse – from cubes to slabs to sticks – can give us the 'picture in the mind' that we need to see decimal numbers getting infinitely small, but still according to a strict, regular pattern.

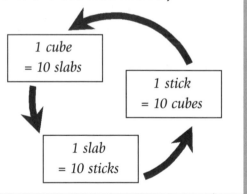

1 cube = 10 slabs

1 stick = 10 cubes

1 slab = 10 sticks

c) Using Symbols to Represent Place Value

We have seen that the key to understanding place value is scale. But the key to understanding the use of numbers and symbols to *represent* place value is *movement*. When *4* is multiplied by *10*, so that it becomes *40*, it *moves*. It moves one place to the left.

But the trouble is, it doesn't. Few teachers would ever actually teach a pupil that they should 'add a nought' to multiply a whole number by ten – but that, in reality, is what happens. If written symbols are used to represent *4 multiplied by 10*, then the teacher may talk about the *4* moving up one place to the left, but to the pupil it is obvious that the *4* stays put. The *0* just takes up its position after it.

| 4 |
| 40 |

Calculators can certainly help here. They do not just 'add a nought' when a whole number is multiplied by 10: they visibly move the number one position to the left. Teachers may hesitate to encourage pupils to use a calculator to do something as 'easy' as multiplying a whole number by 10 – but getting the right answer really is not the point here. The calculator offers a 'picture to think with' which will help to combat pupils' misconceptions about the function of the '0' in this context.

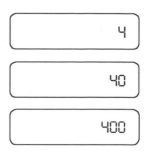

In the Classroom – *Modelling Place Value*

A chart showing how each written number relates to its model will help to give meaning to the written symbols.

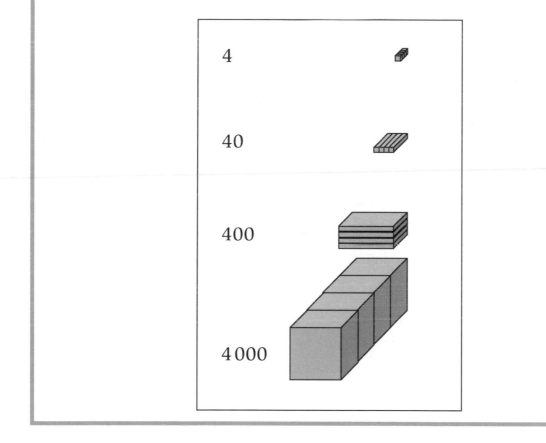

Although it is a valuable tool to help pupils to understand what happens when a whole number is multiplied by 10, with decimal numbers the calculator undermines its own good teaching practice. What appears on the screen when *24.69* is multiplied by 10 is *246.9* Most of the digits are in the same place as before: it is the decimal point that appears to have moved, swapping positions with the *6*. This image does

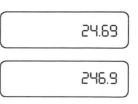

not convey the key concept of the movement of all the digits up one place to the left. So, rather than a calculator, teachers need to use resources and activities that emphasise that the digits move while the decimal point stays put.

In the Classroom – *Place Value and Position*

Arrow Cards or a Place Value Chart (obtainable from www.education-initiatives.co.uk) are useful tools to help pupils to relate the position of a digit to its value.

Pupils can also make a 'folding number', cut out of a sheet of A4 paper, to show how a multi-digit whole number breaks down into its constituent parts. *376*, for instance, breaks down into *300, 70* and *6*, while *444* breaks down into *400, 40* and *4*. See Photocopiable Resource Sheet 5.

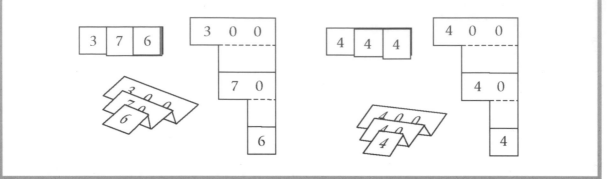

In the Classroom – *The Decimal Slide*

A sliding model which demonstrates the movement of the digits when a decimal number is multiplied or divided by a power of ten can be made out of a sheet of A4 paper. The paper is folded and two windows are cut, with the decimal point between them. Then a 1- or 2-digit number, followed by some 0s, are written on a strip of paper.

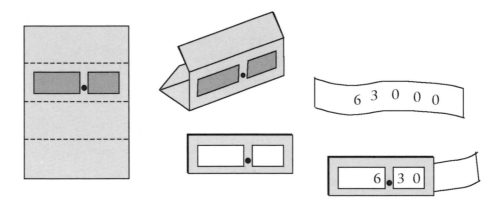

The strip of paper is fed through one end of the folded paper to slide beneath the windows.

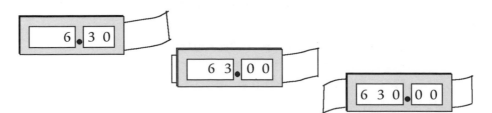

As the strip slides to the left, the number is multiplied by 10: as it slides to the right, it is divided by 10.

See Photocopiable Resource Sheets 6 and 7.

The vital role played by the *0* as a 'place holder' in, say, the number *630* becomes clear with this sliding model. If we did not have the *0* to fill the units column then there would be nothing to distinguish *630* from *63*. Even if the paper strip is too short to show them all, we can imagine a string of *0*s trailing off to the right, ready to slide up as the number on the strip is multiplied by ten again and again. A larger model, and a longer strip, would allow for numbers with more digits – but a model made from a sheet of A4 paper, with two non-zero digits and three zeros, will get the idea across. It will give pupils a visual and kinaesthetic 'picture in the mind' of the movement of the digits across the decimal point that they are far more likely to remember than any number of written exercises on static, printed sheets.

In the Classroom – *Pupil Numbers*

A row of pupils, each holding a card showing one digit of a 'decimal number', stand on either side of a fixed decimal point drawn on a flip chart. On the command 'Multiply by ten', all the pupils move up one place; 'Divide by a hundred' means they must all move down two places; and so on. Other calculations involving a change to a single digit may also be used – so 'subtract ten', for example, means that the pupil currently in the 'tens' position must swap their card for one with a lower value, while 'add three tenths' means that the pupil two places down must display a higher-value card. This activity helps to focus attention on the position of each digit, and on the way this changes depending on the magnitude of the number being displayed.

All the models and activities that teachers can use to explain whole numbers and decimals, and their multiplication and division by powers of ten, have one driving purpose. They all offer a 'picture in the mind' that the pupil can use to make sense of place value. Symbols and rules may mean little in themselves, and are easily forgotten. But once the conventions have meaning, pupils are far more likely to recall and use them effectively.

Place Value and Decimals – Key Points

- The key to understanding place value is **scale**.
- The cycle cubes → sticks → slabs → cubes gives us a 'picture in the mind' of place value at any position in the system.
- A *1 000* cube is the same shape as a *1* cube. It is just on a different scale.
- The model for **4.378** is the same as the model for **4 378**. Again, it is just on a different scale.
- The key to understanding the representation of place value is **movement**.
- When a number is multiplied by 10, the digits move to the left. Every teacher teaches this – but not every pupil learns it!
- The movement should be demonstrated not on static paper, but with a sliding model.

CHAPTER 5

Fractions

- *The 'four rules' for fractions are commonly presented as a set of instructions for manipulating numbers and symbols.*

- *Shapes and patterns may be used to represent fractions, and these will help to give the symbols meaning.*

- *When the symbols have meaning pupils can understand, not just learn, the 'four rules'.*

a) Symbols and Images

The 'four rules' for the manipulation of fractions are some of the most complicated, confusing, and just plain bizarre that are ever inflicted on children in our schools.

> *To add two fractions, you give them a common denominator by multiplying the top and bottom numbers by the same number and then you add the two top numbers and then you cancel down.*

> *To multiply two fractions you multiply the two top numbers together and the two bottom numbers together and then you cancel down.*

> *To divide one fraction by another you turn them upside down … No, you turn the first one … No, the second one … Well, anyway, you turn one of them upside down and then you multiply. Or is it divide? Divide would make more sense … Oh, and then you cancel down. When in doubt, always cancel down. You may get a mark.*

No wonder pupils – even relatively numerate pupils, who can remember the multiplication tables at least some of the time – get confused. For a visual and kinaesthetic learner the whole thing can be a nightmare.

It need not be. Fractions, after all, are just bits of things. They have shape and pattern. They can be understood spatially. But the numbers can get in the way.

The problem with fractions is that, like so much of mathematics, they are usually represented with numbers. So the universal representation of *three quarters*, for example, is $^{3}/_{4}$, not

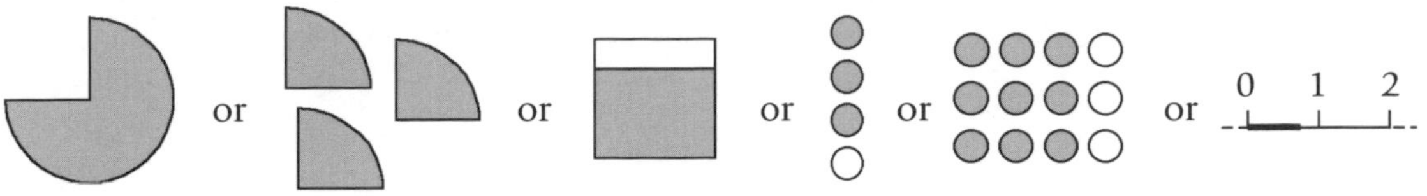

Each of these diagrams offers a possible interpretation of the symbol $^{3}/_{4}$. And like numbers represented on the Slavonic abacus, each one also carries a representation of the complement to the whole – the 'missing' quarter.

The symbol $^{3}/_{4}$ can have any of the interrelated meanings represented by the diagrams, and many more besides – three out of every four of something; forty-five minutes in an hour; the probability of not getting a heart when one card is picked from a pack of fifty-two; and so on. This generality of the symbolic representation makes it very powerful, but it also makes it confusing. All the different meanings of *three quarters*, and the interconnections between them, need to be recognised and discussed – and, as always, represented in a way that can be grasped and recalled by pupils who think more easily in pictures than in words.

b) n nths Make a Whole One

If we want to do anything with the parts that fractions represent – if we want to add or subtract them, for example – then we must first make sure that they are all made up of the same-sized bits. We cannot add

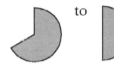

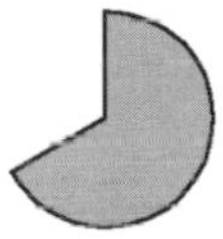 to 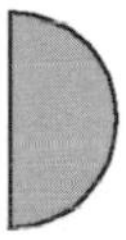

, for instance, because these two fractions are different sizes and shapes. We must first break up the *two thirds* and the *half* into pieces that are all the same size. If we break the *two thirds* into four pieces, and the *half* into three, then all our pieces will be the same size and shape – they will all be *sixths*.

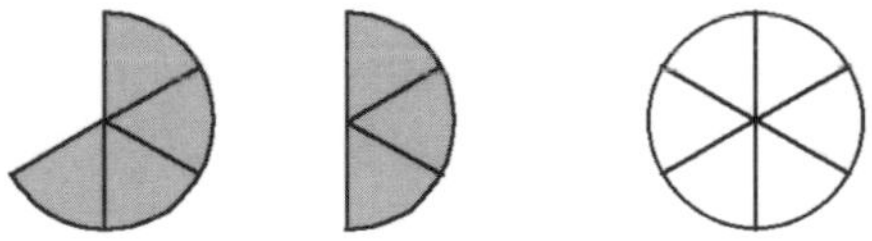

Now all the pieces will fit together properly, because they are all the same size and shape. There are seven of them altogether – four from the *two thirds* and three from the *half* – so the total is *seven sixths*, or *one whole* and *one sixth*.

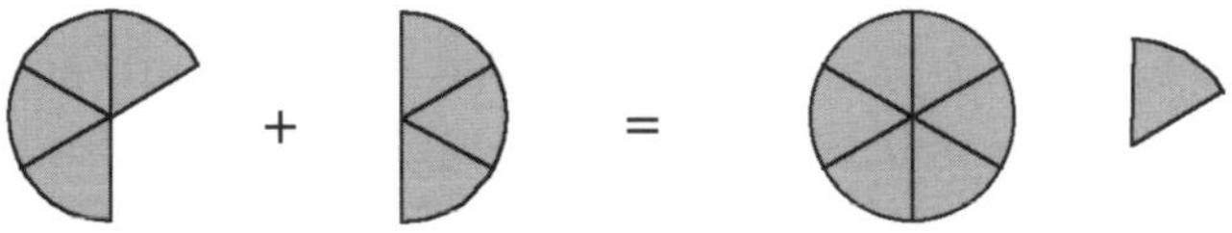

The key concept here, one that that needs to be rehearsed and emphasised in a lot of different contexts, is that *n nths make a whole one*. This applies no matter what constitutes the 'whole one'. It might be a circular 'pie' like the ones illustrated above, or a step one unit long on a number line, or a number of objects – a dozen eggs, say, or a bag of apples. Pupils need plenty of experience of breaking up whole ones into n nths, physically and mentally, so they learn not just *that* $^{1}/_{4}$ is less than $^{1}/_{3}$, and $^{1}/_{96}$ is less than $^{1}/_{57}$, but *why*. There are more quarters than thirds in the whole one, so each quarter must be smaller than a third.

There is evidence that many pupils – not just predominantly visual and kinaesthetic learners – find fractions easier to understand, and to work with, when they are presented as fractions *of* something. This was indicated by the results of a trial to develop a series of age-standardised mathematics tests for pupils in primary and secondary schools. Two groups, with 1 300 pupils aged between 8 and 14 years in each, were given different versions of what was essentially the same question (Clausen-May et al., 2005; Clausen-May and Vappula, 2005). In one version the question was presented graphically, while in the other it was presented only with numbers and symbols.

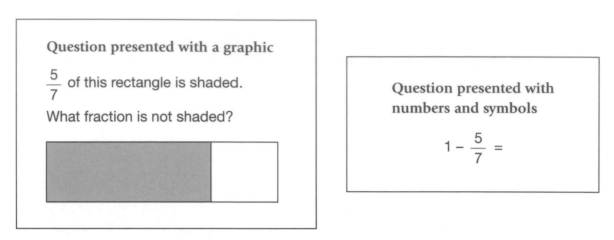

Question presented with a graphic

$\dfrac{5}{7}$ of this rectangle is shaded.

What fraction is not shaded?

Question presented with numbers and symbols

$$1 - \dfrac{5}{7} =$$

In the Classroom – *n nths make a Whole One*

Pupils can make a poster showing examples of shapes divided into a number of equal parts. This will help to reinforce standard exercises on the use of conventional fraction notation.

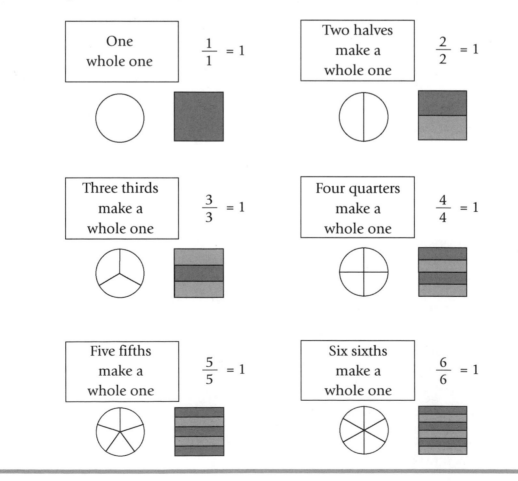

One whole one — $\dfrac{1}{1} = 1$

Two halves make a whole one — $\dfrac{2}{2} = 1$

Three thirds make a whole one — $\dfrac{3}{3} = 1$

Four quarters make a whole one — $\dfrac{4}{4} = 1$

Five fifths make a whole one — $\dfrac{5}{5} = 1$

Six sixths make a whole one — $\dfrac{6}{6} = 1$

The proportion of pupils getting each question correct rose with age, as one would expect. But overall, only 38% of the pupils were able to answer the numerically presented question, while 61% – nearly two thirds as many again – were able to give the correct answer when the question was presented graphically. These results offer a clear demonstration of just how powerful a simple 'model to think with' can be in helping pupils to understand what is going on when they manipulate and calculate with fractions.

c) Calculating with Fractions

Once pupils really understand that there are *n nths in a whole one* they may go on to use the four rules for fractions, using diagrams to *justify* and *explain* each step of the operation. This process of justification and explanation is the basis of mathematical proof. It is relevant at every level and in every area of mathematics, but it is particularly valuable for those topics, of which fractions is a prime example, that are peculiarly prone to teaching and learning by rule-based rote. Children may know *how* to solve a routine problem, but be quite unable to explain *why* the method they are using works. A model or a diagram will very often open the door to the *why*, even for pupils who are, at least for a time, capable of recalling and reproducing the steps for the *how*.

Most text books introduce the four rules for fractions using a diagrammatic approach. For example:

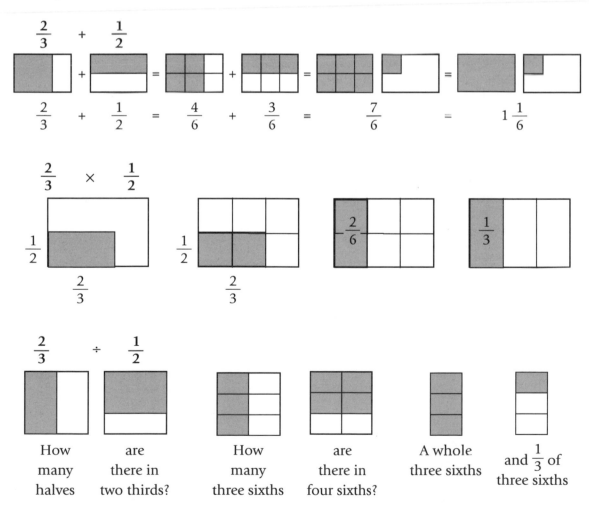

Diagrams like these are certainly helpful to visual and kinaesthetic thinkers. But they are often abandoned much too quickly, before the pupil has had time to establish a 'picture in the mind' on which to hang their understanding, not just of the particular computation involved in the individual question, but of the whole principle of the addition or multiplication of fractions. Instead, they are given rules expressed in words and numbers – which they promptly forget.

But an understanding of the rules for manipulating the symbols can be based on an understanding of the graphics. If the connections between the graphics and the rules are made clear, then pupils who cannot recall the rules but can recall the graphics for a simple example can work out the rest for themselves when they need to.

In each of the tables below, the column on the left shows how the shapes are manipulated for one operation. The column on the right describes the same manipulation, but in terms of numbers and symbols. The aim should be to develop the pupils' understanding of the connections between the two.

So, for example, the picture for the addition or subtraction of fractions is of breaking up two different sized and shaped fractions of a whole in order to fit them together neatly. Finding a common denominator is the numerical and symbolic equivalent of this process.

Adding Fractions

Using Graphics	*Using Rules*
To **add two fractions** of a whole, e.g.	To **add two fractions**, e.g. $\frac{2}{3} + \frac{1}{2}$
you break them up into same-sized bits e.g.	you give them a common denominator by multiplying the numerator and the denominator by the same multiplier e.g. $\frac{4}{6} + \frac{3}{6}$
and then you put the bits together e.g.	and then you add the two numerators e.g. $\frac{7}{6}$
into whole ones and the biggest same-sized bits you can. e.g.	and then you cancel down and make a mixed number. e.g. $1\frac{1}{6}$

For multiplication we use the area model again, just as for the multiplication of whole numbers (see Chapter 3).

Multiplying Fractions

Using Graphics	*Using Rules*
To **multiply two fractions** of a whole, you draw the two fractions of a line, *e.g.*	To **multiply two fractions**, *e.g.* $\dfrac{2}{3} \times \dfrac{1}{2}$
then you draw the rectangle with the two lines as its edges *e.g.*	you multiply the two numerators together and the two denominators together *e.g.* $\dfrac{2 \times 1}{3 \times 2}$
and find its area *e.g.*	*e.g.* $\dfrac{2}{6}$
using the biggest same-sized bits you can. *e.g.* =	and then you cancel down. *e.g.* $\dfrac{1}{3}$

The diagrams for both addition and multiplication lead directly to the standard rules for the addition and multiplication of fractions. The picture for the division of fractions, on the other hand, does not lead to the 'turning upside down' method that pupils are often asked to commit to memory with little or no understanding. It offers a different – and more meaningful – approach.

Dividing Fractions

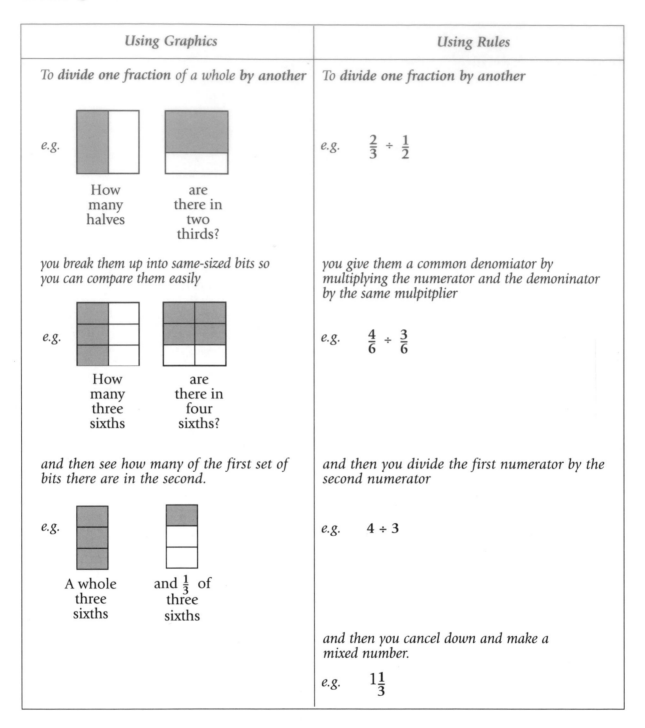

Using Graphics	*Using Rules*
To **divide one fraction** of a whole **by another**	To **divide one fraction by another**
e.g. How many halves / are there in two thirds?	*e.g.* $\frac{2}{3} \div \frac{1}{2}$
you break them up into same-sized bits so you can compare them easily	*you give them a common denomiator by multiplying the numerator and the demoninator by the same mulpitplier*
e.g. How many three sixths / are there in four sixths?	*e.g.* $\frac{4}{6} \div \frac{3}{6}$
and then see how many of the first set of bits there are in the second.	*and then you divide the first numerator by the second numerator*
e.g. A whole three sixths / and $\frac{1}{3}$ of three sixths	*e.g.* $4 \div 3$
	and then you cancel down and make a mixed number.
	e.g. $1\frac{1}{3}$

Using this approach, the two fractions are first *given a common demoninator* (or, in graphical terms, *broken up into the same-sized bits*), just as they are for an addition.

$$^2/_3 \div {}^1/_2$$
$$= {}^4/_6 \div {}^3/_6$$

Now we have a simple division – *How many of the second fraction are there in the first?* Because the two fractions are made up of the same-sized bits they are directly comparable so we are just asking, *How many of the second set of bits do we need to make the first?* or *What is the first set divided by the second?* This translates back into the symbolic and numerical rule, *Divide the first numerator by the second.*

$$^4/_6 \div {}^3/_6$$
$$= 4 \div 3$$

In each case – for addition (or subtraction), multiplication and division, the 'picture in the mind' makes sense of the method. This makes it possible for the visual and kinaesthetic thinker to work out *how* to carry out the calculation by recalling *why* the method works.

d) The Clock Face – Another Useful Model

Another useful model for work with fractions, and one that is connected with other areas of the mathematics curriculum, is the analogue clock face. This is divided into twelve equal sections, conveniently labelled 1 to 12. The minute hand of the clock turns through a quarter turn to the three, and a half turn to the six, to show 'quarter past' and 'half past' the hour. So there we are, even before we have begun to think about fractions, with *three twelfths* and *six twelfths* equal to a *quarter* and a *half* – all from learning to tell the time.

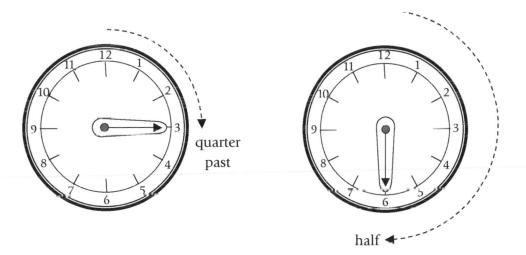

The other fractions on a clock face are not commonly used in the context of time – we do not usually say *three quarters past four* or *one third past seven*. But these, along with sixths and twelfths, may be demonstrated, using an overhead transparency of the clock face and a 'hand' cut out of card and attached with a split-pin paper fastener. The standard analogue clock face is useful only for computations involving halves, thirds, quarters, sixths and twelfths – but these are enough to establish a feel for what it means to add and subtract fractions. Pupils may have their own smaller versions of the clock face with a rotating hand, cut out of card. Photocopiable Resource Sheets 8 and 9 can be used to prepare these materials.

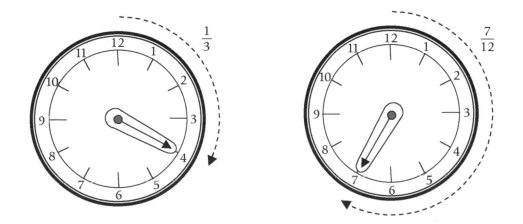

In the Classroom – *Clock-Face Fractions*

The clock face may be used to add and subtract halves, thirds, quarters, sixths and twelfths.

To start with, pupils will need to use the physical model of the clock face for computations like these. But later, when the visual and kinaesthetic 'picture in the mind' has become firmly established, they can learn to work mentally, using a mental image to imagine the clock hand moving around the clock face.

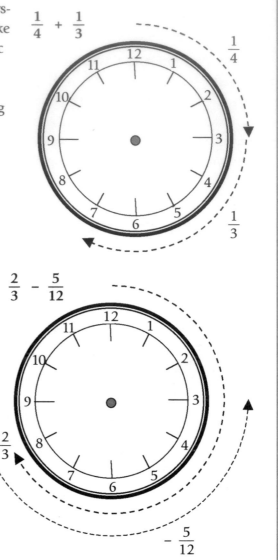

This is a quick and flexible method for the solution of such problems as $^1/_4 + ^1/_3$ or $^2/_3 - ^5/_{12}$, which, like any meaningful piece of mathematics, is much easier to recall than a rote-learnt rule.

Fractions – Key Points

■ Pupils often practise using the 'four rules for fractions' with little understanding.

■ The symbolic representation of a fraction can carry a great range of different meanings, which need to be identified and understood.

■ Pupils who think more easily in pictures than in words need a variety of mental images that they can recall.

■ Diagrams for operations on fractions give the **why** as well as the **how**.

■ The key concept is that **n nths make a whole one**.

■ A useful image for the addition, subtraction and division of fractions is of chopping the fractions up into sets of equal-sized bits which can then be combined or compared directly.

■ The multiplication of fractions can be understood with an area model.

■ A clock face offers another useful model for the addition and subtraction of fractions.

CHAPTER 6

Ratio, Proportion and Percentages

- *Ratio and proportion are usually presented as primarily numerical concepts.*

- *This may make them hard for visual and kinaesthetic thinkers to grasp.*

- *Similar shapes offer a useful 'picture in the mind' for ratio.*

- *The image of 'bundles' may also be used.*

- *The hundred-unit percentage grid brings together fractions, decimals and percentages, and helps to show how these are interrelated.*

a) Picturing Ratios

The concept of ratio is complex. It is normally introduced in the context of relationships between sets of numbers, rather than lengths or shapes – but this may make it more confusing for pupils who think more readily in pictures than in words and symbols. Pupils are expected to understand the idea of a *ratio* between two numbers, such as *two to three*, long before they meet the concept of a pair of *similar shapes*, one of which is an enlargement of the other. For visual and kinaesthetic thinkers, this may be the wrong way round.

For example, take a purely numerical problem:

If two pounds are worth three Euros, what are four pounds worth?

This may be represented as:

2:3 = 4:?

There are four numbers to think about here – three given, and one to find. The pupil must realise that the relationship between the *2* and the *3* is the same as the relationship between the *4* and the *?*, and that the relationship between the *2* and the *4* is the same as the relationship between the *3* and the *?*, but the relationship between the *3* and the *4*, or the *2* and the *?*, is irrelevant. Working out which relationship is which, and which ones matter, is difficult. They are, after all, just a lot of numbers. It is not obvious which 'go together', or why.

But if, instead, the problem relates to a pair of mathematically similar shapes, then the numbers may make better sense. For example, if the numerical problem *2:3 = 4:?* is presented in the context of a pair of rectangles, then the first rectangle has a height

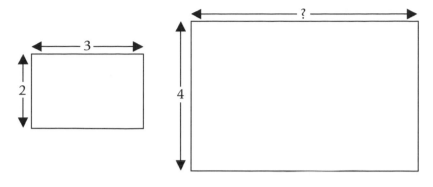

of 2 units and a width of 3 units. The second rectangle is exactly the same shape as the first. It is just bigger. It is twice as high as the smaller rectangle, but it has not changed its shape. It has just grown steadily. So if it is twice as high, then it must also be twice as wide.

Now the important relationships – the pairs of numbers that 'go together' – can be identified from the rectangles. The width of the first rectangle is one and a half times its height – so the second rectangle must also have a width that is one and a half times its height. That is, the relationship between the 2 and the 3 (the ratio 2:3) must be the same as the relationship between the 4 and the ? (the ratio 4:?). Again, the height of the second rectangle is twice the height of the first, so the width of the second rectangle must also be twice the width of the first. That is, the relationship between the 2 and the 4 (the ratio 2:4) must be the same as the relationship between the 3 and the ? (the ratio 3:?). Either way I can get a feel for the size of the ?, before I calculate it more exactly as 6. If we change the height of any rectangle then we must also change its width, or it will distort and become a different shape. But there is clearly no reason to focus on the relationship between the 3 and the 4, or between the 2 and the ?, because this would involve comparing the width of one rectangle with the height of the other.

In the Classroom – *Similar shapes*

The model of a shape that 'grows' but does not distort may be reinforced with plenty of graphical examples.

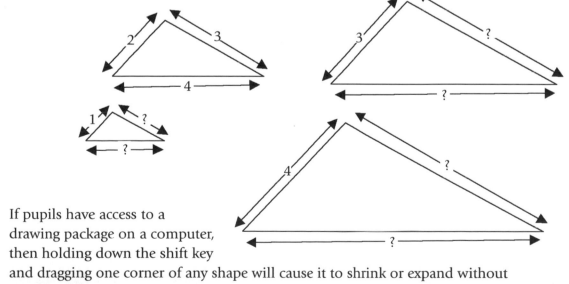

If pupils have access to a drawing package on a computer, then holding down the shift key and dragging one corner of any shape will cause it to shrink or expand without distorting. This moving image provides a vivid 'picture in the mind' on which pupils may base their understanding of ratio.

b) Proportion

Another useful image to help pupils to picture ratio and proportion is the idea of 'bundles'. The problem *2:3 = 4:?* may be represented with 'bundles' of two – with two bundles of, say, white cubes, and three bundles of grey. This gives two white to three grey *bundles*, but it also gives four white to six grey *cubes*. If each of the bundles contained more cubes then there could be six white to nine grey cubes, or twenty white to thirty grey cubes, or whatever, but there would still be only two white to three grey bundles, so all these ratios are equivalent.

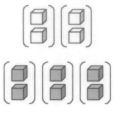

This image is particularly useful in helping pupils to understand the concept of proportion, and its connection with *fraction of*. The terms *ratio* and *proportion* go together, but they mean different things. A *proportion* is out of the whole, while a *ratio* is of one part to another. The picture of the bundles of cubes allows us to use the different terms in a way that brings out their connected meanings.

> *There are 2 white cubes for every 3 grey cubes.*
>
> *There are 3 grey cubes for every 2 white cubes.*
>
> *The ratio of white cubes to grey cubes is 2 to 3, or 2:3.*
>
> *The ratio of grey cubes to white cubes is 3 to 2, or 3:2.*
>
> *The proportion of white cubes is 2 out of 5. $^2/_5$ of the cubes are white.*
>
> *The proportion of grey cubes is 3 out of 5. $^3/_5$ of the cubes are grey.*

The image of the bundles of cubes may seem easier to understand than the similar rectangles. An example like this, perhaps involving bundles of apples and pears, or the ingredients for a recipe, rather than different colours of cubes, is common in primary mathematics text books. But the bundles model is heavily dependent on numbers, and it may, for that reason, be less appropriate as an introduction to ratio and proportion for pupils who find numbers difficult to comprehend. The image of a shape, growing or shrinking but never distorting, is easier to manipulate mentally. I can make a shape grow, or shrink, in one easy movement. The kinaesthetic experience is smooth and comfortable. On the other hand, the bundles showing the connection

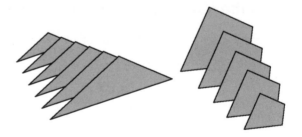

between the ratios twelve to sixteen, eighteen to twenty-four, and three to four, for example, are more fiddly. I am likely to lose track of the difference between the numbers of bundles (the *3:4*) and the numbers of white and grey cubes (the *12:16* and the *18:24*) in the picture. Shapes that grow and shrink offer a more holistic model. This may help visual and kinaesthetic learners to grasp the principle of ratio without having to worry about specific numbers of cubes and bundles.

12:16 = 3:4

18:24 = 3:4

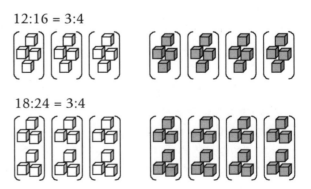

In the Classroom – *Maps and Scale*

Maps and scale models provide a useful context for the development of pupils' understanding of proportion.

A series of maps or aerial photographs, each covering the position of the school at a different scale, will convey a sense of 'zooming in' which can help pupils to develop an understanding of scale. These could range from a plan of the solar system or a satellite picture on a very small scale, through a selection of maps or photographs to a large-scale plan or photograph of the classroom. Maps centring on the school may be downloaded and printed off from the web (www.streetmap.co.uk).

Some pupils may find it interesting to consider how some dolls are distorted, while others are fairly accurate scale models. It is commonly reported that if a Barbie doll were a full-size woman, she would be six feet tall and, at 101 pounds, seriously underweight (www.anred.com/stats.html). What conclusions may be drawn about other dolls?

A collection of cereal boxes, from the 'individual portion' to the 'giant' 750 gram or 1 kilo size, can present an interesting problem. Are all the boxes the same shape (that is, mathematically similar), or do they distort as they change size?

c) Percentages

A percentage is a proportion. It is what a fraction would be if it were out of a hundred. So to convert a fraction to a percentage we must divide the whole up into a hundred parts. This can be represented with a hundred-unit percentage grid superimposed on the whole.

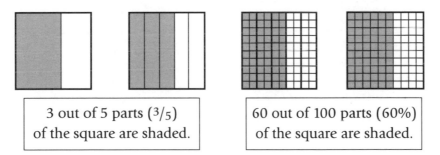

| 3 out of 5 parts ($^3/_5$) of the square are shaded. | 60 out of 100 parts (60%) of the square are shaded. |

But the problem with converting many fractions into percentages is that they do not map easily onto a proportion of a hundred. When the fraction is a proportion of a factor or a multiple of a hundred it is not too difficult. The hundred-unit percentage grid can be manipulated to fit neatly over the parts of the original fraction. So 9 out of 25, for example, can be seen as 36 out of a hundred, or 36%.

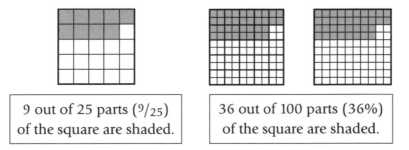

| 9 out of 25 parts ($^9/_{25}$) of the square are shaded. | 36 out of 100 parts (36%) of the square are shaded. |

Similarly, a proportion of 200 can be represented by stretching the percentage grid out to show that each 'one per cent' covers 2 out of the 200.

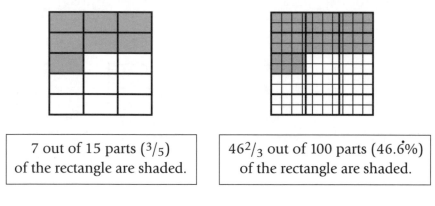

| 135 out of 200 parts ($^{135}/_{200}$) of the rectangle are shaded. | 67$^1/_2$ out of 100 parts (67.5%) of the rectangle are shaded. |

But a hundred does not have many factors. Compared to 144, say, or 360, it has very few. Many real problems involve proportions that cannot be represented by whole number percentages – that is, by a whole number 'out of a hundred'. Hampered as we are with ten fingers and thumbs, our number system is inevitably clumsy because the base we use is not easily divisible by anything but multiples of 2 or 5. When the fraction to be converted is not a factor or a multiple of a hundred it can be difficult to 'see' how the hundred-unit percentage grid can be made to fit over it.

The picture for 7 out of 15, for example, is more complicated. The hundred units of the percentage grid will not fit neatly over the fifteenths in the fraction. Forty-six of the unit squares are covered completely, but an odd third of each of two unit squares in the percentage grid have to be added together to give $^2/_3$, or 0.$\dot{6}$.

| 7 out of 15 parts ($^3/_5$) of the rectangle are shaded. | 46$^2/_3$ out of 100 parts (46.$\dot{6}$%) of the rectangle are shaded. |

And even a common, straightforward fraction like $^1/_3$ gives an awkward, 'bitty' picture which leads to a fraction or a repeating decimal in the equivalent percentage.

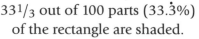

| 1 out of 3 parts ($^1/_3$) of the rectangle are shaded. | 33$^1/_3$ out of 100 parts (33.$\dot{3}$%) of the rectangle are shaded. |

Here there are ten odd thirds that have to be combined to make 3$\frac{1}{3}$, which must then be added to the 30 unit squares that are completely shaded in the hundred-unit percentage grid.

So the concept of a percentage may be difficult for visual and kinaesthetic thinkers to grasp. They may understand that, when using a percentage, they are expressing a proportion out of a hundred rather than out of some other convenient whole number. *Per cent*, after all, means *per hundred – out of a hundred*. Using a common denominator – that is, splitting each of the 'wholes' into the same number of parts – makes it easy to compare the relative sizes of the different fractions. But a hundred is a clumsy number to use to divide up the wholes. Its use is a matter of convention, leading directly from our decimal number system, but it is likely to cause pupils who think more easily in pictures and models than in words and symbols some difficulty. It is not easy to create the visual and kinaesthetic 'pictures in the mind' needed to think effectively about percentages.

d) Making Links – Fractions, Percentages and Decimals

Most mathematics textbooks have a table showing the equivalences between some common fractions, decimals and percentages. There may be a poster displayed in the classroom showing some of these number facts. But what these tables and posters lack is any explanation of the *why* that underlies the *how*. Here again, we need a picture that will link together the three concepts – fractions, decimals and percentages. It is not

$\frac{1}{4}$	$\frac{3}{10}$	$\frac{1}{3}$
0.25	0.3	0.$\dot{3}$
25%	30%	33.$\dot{3}$%

immediately obvious, for example, what $\frac{1}{4}$ has to do with 25%. The two symbolic representations do not have a single squiggle in common. But a simple diagram can make the connection clear.

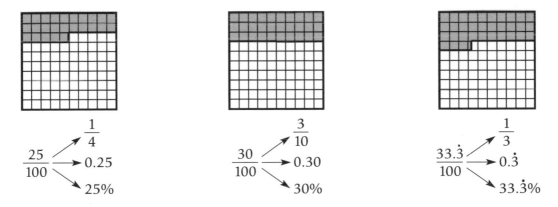

The key here is in the use of the hundred-unit square. The poster stating the equivalences may seem to summarise what the diagrams show – but to visual and kinaesthetic learners it is the diagrams, rather than the lists of symbols, that summarise each set of relationships.

is meaningful and memorable, but $\frac{1}{4} = 0.25 = 25\%$ is not.

As always, the focus, at least for the spatial thinkers in the classroom, must be on developing their understanding of the relationships. Then even if they cannot recall the equivalences, they will have a way to work these out for themselves.

In the Classroom – *Making Links*

Pupils can make a series of posters, each one based on a partially shaded hundred square, with the shading expressed as a fraction out of a hundred, a fraction in its lowest terms, a decimal and a percentage. Where the percentage is a whole number it may also be shown on the Slavonic abacus.

Ratio, Proportion and Percentages – Key Points

- For visual and kinaesthetic thinkers, the concept of mathematical similarity holds the key to understanding ratio.

- Images of 'bundles' are useful to bring out the relationship between ratio and proportion.

- A percentage is a 'proportion out of a hundred'.

- It can be difficult to see how the whole will split into a hundred parts, so percentages may be difficult for spatial thinkers to visualise and understand.

- The image of a shaded hundred square can serve to bring out the links between equivalent fractions, decimals and percentages.

Algebra

- *Algebra is, by its very nature, symbolic.*

- *The algebraic x is used in different ways.*

- *The image of a balancing scale may be used to establish the meaning of the equality sign.*

- *Meaningful algebraic expressions may be developed from patterns.*

a) Using Symbols

Algebra is full of symbols. The quintessential algebraic symbol for most people – adults as well as children – is x. x crops up all over the place, with different meanings and different values in different situations. This can be very confusing.

x can represent one or more specific values in an equation. These values are (at least to begin with) unknown, but it may be possible to work out what they are – so x is 6 in $4 + x = 10$, for example, but it is 3 or -3 in $x^2 = 9$. x has different values in different equations, but only one, or a limited set, in any one equation.

But x can also represent the variable in a function. You can choose different values for x, and these will produce different outputs. So in the function $y = x + 3$, for example, y is 4 when x is 1, but y is 96 when x is 93.

These two uses of x, in an equation where it has a specific, unknown value, and in a function where it serves as a variable that can take different values, need to be understood. So for early work in algebra the first thing we need is a symbol that indicates clearly, in itself, the range of meanings and values that x can have. Some textbooks use a box for the unknown when equations are introduced, with $4 + \square = 10$, for example, or $\square - 7 = 2$. This is helpful, as the boxes are closed so we do not know what is inside, but we may be able to open them to find out. The variable in a function, on the other hand, may be thought of as a box into which we can put a range of values – so in $\blacksquare = \square + 3$ we have a function relating the variable $\blacksquare$ to the variable $\square$, where the number in $\blacksquare$ is always three more than the number in $\square$. Then, with time, the more conventional letters can be introduced.

b) Solving Equations – the Balancing Model

The equality sign has a very clear meaning. It means that the total value of everything on one side of the '=' is equal to the total value of everything on the other side.

That, at least, is the theory. But what many pupils understand by the equality sign is the instruction: *Work out the answer*. They meet thousands of such orders over a period of years in exercises set out with an equality sign and an answer space:

$3 + 6 =$ _____ ; $4 \times 9 + 17 =$ _____ ; $16\pi - \sqrt{(3.6)} =$ _____ ; $(x + 3)(x + 1) =$ _____ ;

and so on. In each case, the equality sign actually carries the message *Do the calculation on the left, and write the answer on the right*. This can lead to such nonsensical working as:

$4 \times 9 + 17 = 4 \times 9 = 36 + 17 = 53$

The real meaning of the equality sign should be discussed early, before the introduction of formal algebra. The visual and kinaesthetic 'picture in the mind' that we need here is a well-established one, and it is very effective. It shows a set of balancing scales, which must be kept balanced by ensuring that the total value of everything in each of the two pans is equal.

This image is very powerful. If it is firmly established early on it will help to discourage pupils from representing a series of non-equivalent expressions as though they were all equal, as in the nonsensical working above. Since there is a pan on each side the equivalences work

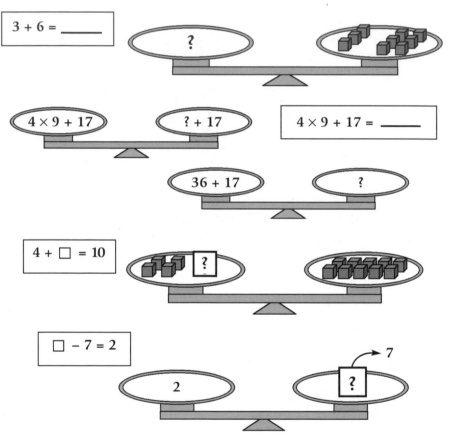

both ways, giving both 3 + 6 = 9, and 9 = 3 + 6. The former represents the aggregation of two groups, and the latter a partitioning of a whole number. The concept of the balance helps to discourage the use of meaningless rules for algebraic manipulation, such as *Change sides, change sign*. As always, it is the meaning that underlies the symbols that must be the focus of attention, not a set of rules for their manipulation.

c) Writing Expressions

Just as numbers may be understood holistically, as patterns of dots on a Slavonic abacus, so algebraic expressions may be given a graphical meaning that will help pupils who think more easily in pictures than in words and symbols to understand and work with them effectively.

In the Classroom – *Writing Simple Algebraic Expressions*

Pupils can use a set of shapes with given areas to make simple patterns, then express the total areas of their patterns algebraically.

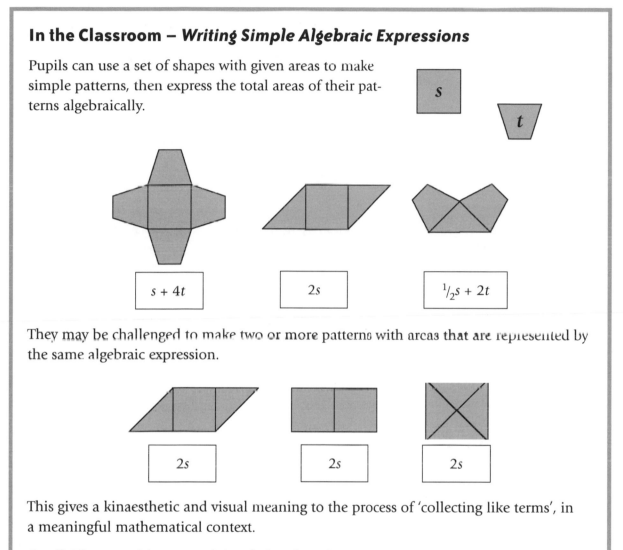

They may be challenged to make two or more patterns with areas that are represented by the same algebraic expression.

This gives a kinaesthetic and visual meaning to the process of 'collecting like terms', in a meaningful mathematical context.

Geoff Giles uses this approach in *Algebra through Geometry*, a DIME resource available from Tarquin Publications (www.tarquinbooks.com).

A series of patterns that grow according to a regular rule offers a useful context for writing a meaningful generalised expression. The algebraic expression for the nth member of the series can be pulled directly out of the patterns. The series can start simply, but combine and build up to more elaborate patterns which are represented by complex, but still meaningful, expressions.

In the Classroom – *Generalised Expressions from Series*

Pupils can make a series of simple patterns of counters, then use this as a basis for more complex patterns. For example, Pattern n in this series is made of n^2 counters.

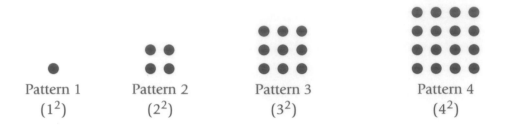

Pattern 1	Pattern 2	Pattern 3	Pattern 4
(1^2)	(2^2)	(3^2)	(4^2)

Adding 4 counters to each pattern gives a related series. Pattern n in this series is made of $n^2 + 4$ counters.

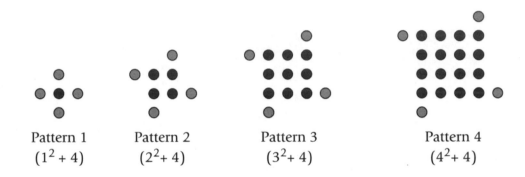

Pattern 1	Pattern 2	Pattern 3	Pattern 4
$(1^2 + 4)$	$(2^2 + 4)$	$(3^2 + 4)$	$(4^2 + 4)$

Or we can double up on the original series, to get a series of patterns made with $2n^2$ counters.

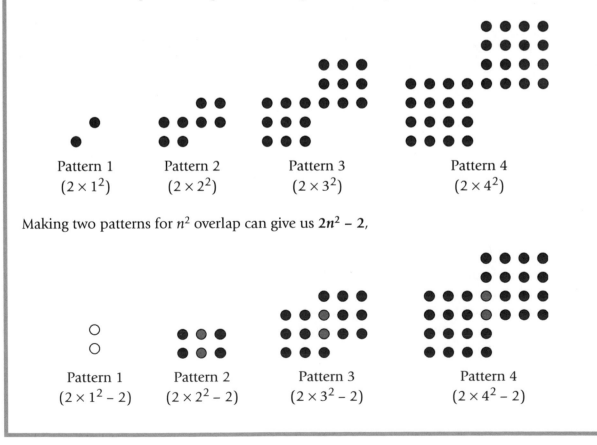

Pattern 1	Pattern 2	Pattern 3	Pattern 4
(2×1^2)	(2×2^2)	(2×3^2)	(2×4^2)

Making two patterns for n^2 overlap can give us $2n^2 - 2$,

Pattern 1	Pattern 2	Pattern 3	Pattern 4
$(2 \times 1^2 - 2)$	$(2 \times 2^2 - 2)$	$(2 \times 3^2 - 2)$	$(2 \times 4^2 - 2)$

or $2n^2 - n$.

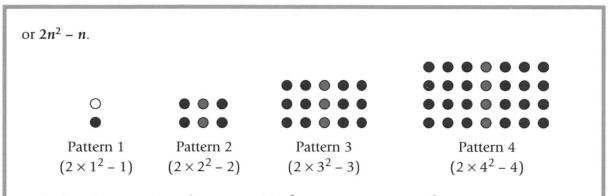

Pattern 1
$(2 \times 1^2 - 1)$

Pattern 2
$(2 \times 2^2 - 2)$

Pattern 3
$(2 \times 3^2 - 3)$

Pattern 4
$(2 \times 4^2 - 4)$

And what about a series of patterns with $n^2 - 2n$ counters? Or $2n^2 - 3n + 4$? The possibilities are endless – but each expression, no matter how complex, has meaning when it is used to express the number of counters in the nth member of a series of patterns.

If algebraic expressions mean something, then the rules for algebraic manipulation will make much more sense. A series of patterns can be shaded in different ways to show why two expressions which look very different may be equivalent. For example, the counters in the series of patterns:

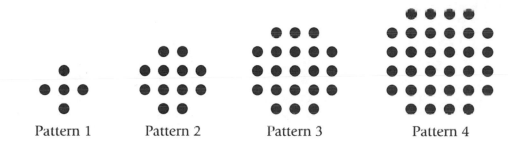

Pattern 1   Pattern 2   Pattern 3   Pattern 4

may be coloured to show that Pattern n in the series has $n^2 + 4n$ counters:

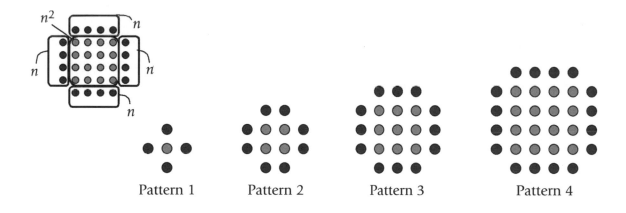

Pattern 1   Pattern 2   Pattern 3   Pattern 4

Alternatively, they may be coloured to show that it has $n(n + 2) + 2n$ counters:

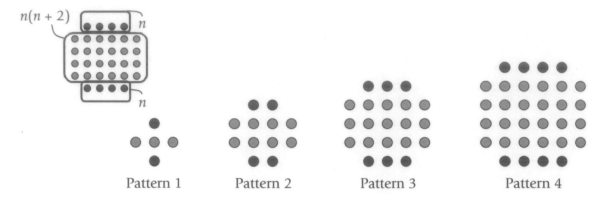

| Pattern 1 | Pattern 2 | Pattern 3 | Pattern 4 |

Or, with attention drawn to the 'missing' counters in the corners, the number of counters in Pattern n can be seen to be $(n + 2)^2 - 4$:

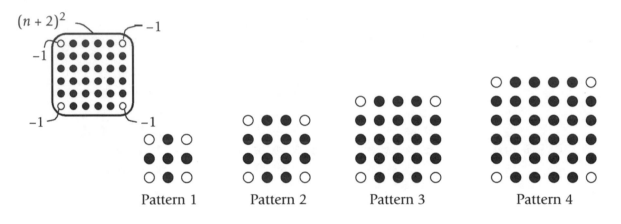

| Pattern 1 | Pattern 2 | Pattern 3 | Pattern 4 |

These diagrams are a graphical representation of the algebraic equivalences,

$$n^2 + 4n = n(n + 2) + 2n = (n + 2)^2 - 4.$$

In each case, the expression can be pulled directly out of the structure of the series of patterns. Each part of the expression can be related back to the relevant sections of the pattern, to give it a meaning that can be seen and understood.

d) Multiplying Algebraic Expressions

We have seen how the physical and spatial concept of the *area of a rectangle* can help pupils to put meaning into both single-digit and long multiplication (see Chapter 3). The same approach may be used to explain what we are doing when we multiply two fractions (see Chapter 5). Now this invaluable 'picture in the mind' makes another appearance, as we come to multiply a pair of algebraic expressions.

Algebraic expressions may be multiplied out sequentially, taking pairs of terms, one from each expression, in turn. For example:

$$(x + 3)(x + 1) = x^2 + x + 3x + 3 = x^2 + 4x + 3$$

Provided pupils keep track of the pairs of terms this will generally lead to the right answer. But it may leave pupils unsure as to why the method works. It may be clear where the x^2 comes from – after all, the x in one bracket has been multiplied by the x in the other. But why does the final expression contain all those loose xs? What do they mean? How are they different from the x^2?

Finding the area of a rectangle with sides of length $(x + 3)$ and $(x + 1)$ gives meaning to the whole process.

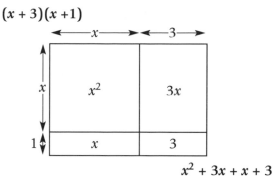

$(x + 3)(x + 1)$

$x^2 + 3x + x + 3$

The expressions to be multiplied out may be more complex – for example:

$(3n + 4)(2n + 2)$

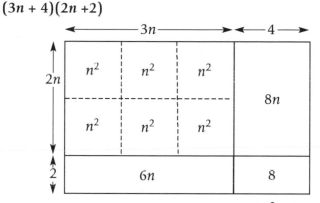

$6n^2 + 8n + 6n + 8$

If there are negative signs in the expressions then it is helpful to think in stages. For example, to find the area of a rectangle with sides of length $(a + 6)$ and $(a - 2)$, we first find the area of a rectangle with sides of length $(a + 6)$ and (a),

$(a + 6)(a - 2)$

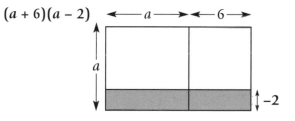

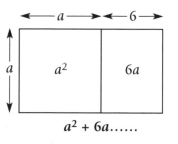

$a^2 + 6a \ldots\ldots$

and then we 'strip off' a rectangle with sides of length $(a + 6)$ and 2.

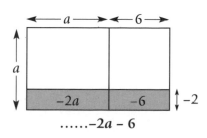

$\ldots\ldots -2a - 6$

Similarly, to find the area of a rectangle with sides of length $(m - 3)$ and $(m - 4)$,

$(m - 3)(m - 4)$

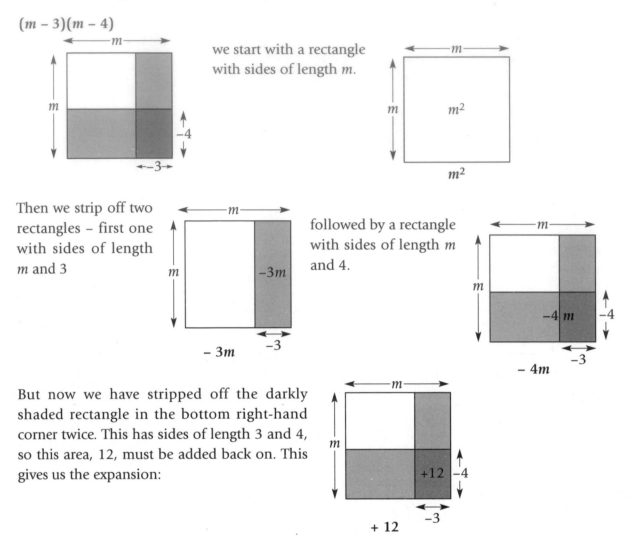

we start with a rectangle with sides of length m.

Then we strip off two rectangles – first one with sides of length m and 3

followed by a rectangle with sides of length m and 4.

But now we have stripped off the darkly shaded rectangle in the bottom right-hand corner twice. This has sides of length 3 and 4, so this area, 12, must be added back on. This gives us the expansion:

$(m - 3)(m - 4) = m^2$ (the m by m square, with nothing stripped off)

      $- 3m$ (the 3 by m rectangle stripped off)

      $- 4m$ (the 4 by m rectangle stripped off)

      $+ 12$ (the doubly-stripped 3 by 4 rectangle replaced.)

The series of diagrams, like those for the previous calculations, not only enable us to expand a pair of brackets, but also to see where each term in the expansion comes from. Why are the terms in m negative? Because we stripped these rectangles away from the m by m square that we started with. Why is the final numerical term positive? Because we have to put back what we have stripped off twice. The whole thing makes sense.

But here again, as so often in mathematics, understanding what is going on takes longer and is more demanding than simply learning a method to get the right answer. The so-called 'boxes method' – see below – may help some pupils to keep track of the steps in the calculation, but it will do little to enable them to understand what they are doing. This example serves to demonstrate how easily an approach designed to foster pupils' understanding of key mathematical concepts can be corrupted into yet another set of 'rules' for getting 'right answers' – meaningless, irrelevant, and altogether forgettable!

☹ NOT to be used – *The 'Boxes' Method*

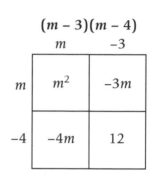

The area approach to the multiplication of two algebraic expressions can be corrupted quite easily into just another routine – the so-called 'boxes' method. This is nothing more than a way of laying out the computation. It does not show why both the terms in m are negative, nor why the '12' is positive. If anything, it is likely to prove more confusing than the linear layout, as it seems to suggest that all the 'boxes' are the same size, and that three of them have one or more negative edge lengths. This method is more cumbersome, and takes longer to draw, than the conventional 'pairing off' routine. It has little to recommend it – and it will certainly not offer a 'picture in the mind' that will support pupils' understanding of the principles that underlie the process of multiplying a pair of algebraic expressions.

Algebra – Key Points

- An algebraic x can have two different uses: as the unknown in an equation, or as a variable in a function. These different uses need to be understood.

- The equality sign, $=$, means that the total value of everything on one side of the symbol is equal to the total value of everything on the other. It does **not** mean 'Do this sum'.

- The balancing model is a valuable 'picture in the mind' to help pupils to understand the meaning of the equality sign.

- Simple patterns and growing series can give meaning to simple and generalised algebraic expressions.

- The area model is once again useful in helping pupils to understand what happens when a pair of algebraic expressions are multiplied together.

CHAPTER 8

Shape, Space and Measures

- *Diagrams and models form the basis of Shape, Space and Measures, but the static limitations of the printed page often dominate the curriculum.*

- *'Mathematical' vocabulary hides, instead of revealing, meaning.*

- *Key concepts in Shape, Space and Measures are often reduced to a set of formulas.*

- *'Pictures in the mind' can enable pupils to re-create concepts and formulas when they need them.*

a) Vocabulary

School mathematics is steeped in hard words. Nowhere is this more evident than in the Shape, Space and Measures curriculum. Mathematical language may present a major hurdle to pupils who could otherwise fly with the ideas and images of shape and space, causing them instead to crash on the mass of mathematical jargon. *Kilogram*, *perimeter*, *pentagon* … these are all hard words, although they refer to quite straightforward ideas.

It is worth spending time making as much sense as possible out of the jargon, de-mystifying it wherever you can. *Pentagon*, for example, is simply the Greek for *five sides*. Talking in Greek is no more mathematically correct than talking in English – so *pentagon* is not a more mathematical term than *five sides*. Our use of Greek in the mathematics classroom is just a historical accident – and it is not helpful to pupils who may find it harder to remember the new word than to understand what it means in the first place.

Pupils need to learn a lot of mathematical jargon in order to achieve under our curriculum. However, it is important always to keep a clear distinction between the mathematical concepts that need to be understood, and the vocabulary used to describe them. So, for example, pupils may identify pairs of shapes that are exactly the same, and others that are the same shape but different sizes, long before they learn the 'mathematical' terms *congruent* and *similar*. Some pupils may succeed in such mathematical activities but struggle to get started in vocabulary-heavy tasks. Mathematical terminology may form a barrier for these pupils, and they are likely to engage with the subject better if they are presented with some activities that do not contain such linguistic hurdles.

In the Classroom – *Metric Measures*

The system of metric measures has the advantage that it is consistent, so there are not, in fact, very many new words to learn. The word *kilo*, for example, just means a *thousand*, whether it be a *kilo-gram*, a *kilo-metre*, or a *kilo-litre*. Pupils may be invited to invent their own uses of *kilo* – so a *kilo-tree*, for instance, might be a wood with a thousand trees, or a *kilo-book*, a library with a thousand books. What could we mean by a *kilo-pupil*, or a *kilo-smile*?

Posters headed 'Hard Words, Easy Ideas', illustrating the concepts and offering a simple, straightforward translation of so-called 'mathematical' terms may help pupils to understand, and so to remember, the words they need. Some pupils may also find it helpful to associate words with movements. If you are fortunate enough to have a hearing-impaired pupil who uses Sign in the classroom, then they might be willing to demonstrate some of the signs they use for 'mathematical' terms. These are often far more meaningful than the accepted spoken and written words. Alternatively, pupils might create their own movements which convey the meanings of mathematical terms that they find hard to remember, and practise saying the words while carrying out the movements.

b) Area and Perimeter

Two concepts that are often introduced together are *area* and *perimeter*. Pupils spend time drawing shapes on squared paper, and counting and recording the number of squares used (the area), and the number of units around the edge (the perimeter). But this approach focuses on the numbers – and to a visual and kinaesthetic thinker one number is very like another, so *area* and *perimeter* are likely to get muddled.

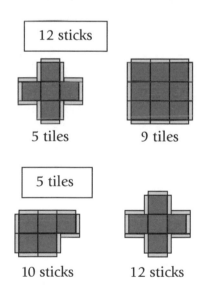

12 sticks

5 tiles   9 tiles

5 tiles

10 sticks   12 sticks

Activities that relate *area* and *perimeter* to different materials may provide a firmer foundation than mere counting for the development of these concepts. Square tiles, which can be picked up and moved around, provide a better starting point for area than drawn squares. A set of sticks that are the same length as the edge of a tile provide a model of the perimeter. The challenge may then be set to surround a given number of tiles with different numbers of sticks, or to fill a space surrounded by a given number of sticks with different numbers of tiles. This is mathematically equivalent to finding sets of shapes with the same area but different perimeters, or the same perimeter but different areas – but it focuses on the common values of the area or the perimeter, not on the words.

This is certainly not a new type of activity. Shapes made with squares joined together edge-to-edge are called *polyominoes* – like *dominoes*, which are made with two squares, but with 'many' (*poly*) instead of 'two'. Simply finding lots of different polyominoes made with different numbers of square tiles is a valuable activity in itself. Finding their areas and perimeters is a natural development. But using square tiles and unit sticks will help pupils to focus distinctly on the two different measures, area and perimeter. In time they may well switch to the conventional drawings on squared paper – but the memory and feel of the square tiles and the sticks will help them to keep sight of the meaning of the different measures they are using.

In the Classroom – *Area and perimeter Scatter Graph*

A scatter graph may be used to develop pupils' understanding of the relationship between area and perimeter. Shapes made with different numbers of squares (*polyominoes*) may be cut out, and stuck onto a large graph with *Perimeter* along the x-axis and *Area* along the y-axis.

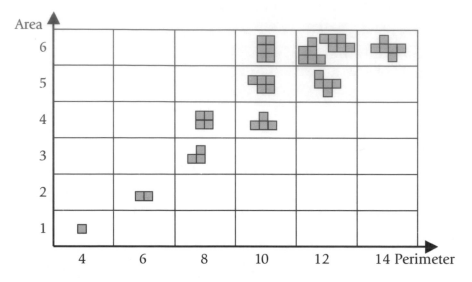

This representation can encourage pupils to ask more questions –

What is the greatest/smallest number of tiles that can be used to make a polyomino with a given perimeter? What is the greatest/smallest perimeter of a polyomino made with a given number of tiles?

Other ways to develop this activity, and its use in assessment for learning, can be found in Clausen-May (2003).

In the Classroom – *Vocabulary: Area and Perimeter*

The 'mathematical' terms *area* and *perimeter* may become easier to remember if they are associated with appropriate movements.

Area is a measure of flatness. A common sign for area is a hand held flat above the table, and moved round in a horizontal plane as if to smooth the air underneath.

A perimeter is the distance around a shape. The common sign for this uses both hands. The forefinger of the left hand is held up, and then a roughly square path is sketched out in the air with the forefinger of the right hand.

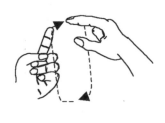

A CD showing signs for a wide range of mathematical terms, *Signs for Education – Mathematics*, is available from Microbooks Ltd, at www.microbooks.org. These may be useful for any pupil who finds it easier to remember meaningful movements than arbitrary words.

c) Models for Formulas

School mathematics is riddled with 'procedures', which pupils may be expected to learn, remember and apply. Shape, Space and Measures is as badly affected in this respect as any other area of the curriculum. Test and examination papers commonly include a Formula Sheet, in which all the pupil's understanding of the concepts of area and volume is reduced to a set of rules. Even when this sheet is not provided, pupils may still be taught the formulas by rote, rather than developing an understanding of the mathematics that underlies them. Then, of course, they forget them.

So here again, pupils who think more easily in pictures than in words and symbols need 'models to think with'. The models make sense, so they are memorable – unlike the formulas. And having remembered the relevant model, the 'picture in the mind', the pupil can work out the formula they need for the problem they are working on.

The first formula pupils are likely to meet is for the area of a rectangle. They start by finding the areas of small rectangles by counting squares – that is, by yet more sequential recitation of disconnected number words. This follows logically from the standard introduction to Number, relying heavily on counting, that was discussed in Chapter 2, but it is less helpful for pupils who see the whole picture at once. On the other hand, visualising a rectangle, and finding its area, lies at the heart of the area model of multiplication discussed in Chapter 3. Pupils who see the calculation 3×4, for example, as

have no need of a formula. They already understand the relationship between the edge lengths and the area of a rectangle on which the formula is based.

The area of a parallelogram can be worked out directly from the area of a rectangle. The parallelogram can be cut into pieces, then reconstructed into a rectangle.

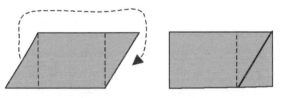

Alternatively, a possibly more memorable model can be made from a stack of cards, such as playing cards or off-cuts from a print shop, formed into a block.

An elastic band holds the stack together, but allows it to be sheared one way or the other. The front face of the stack, which was a rectangle, is transformed by the shearing into a parallelogram with the same height and base.

It also has same area as the original rectangle, as no cards have been added or removed. With this kinaesthetic and visual 'picture in the mind' on which to base their thinking, pupils can see how

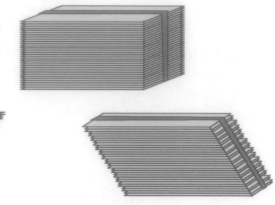

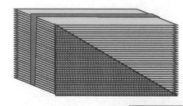

any parallelogram can be sheared back into a rectangle with the same base length, height and area.

Using the same model, a diagonal line and some shading drawn on the other side of the stack will help pupils to perceive a right-angled triangle as half of a rectangle. Any other triangle can then be seen as a shearing of a right-angled triangle with the same base length, height and area.

A different stack, made of thin tiles rather than cards, offers a model from which the area of a trapezium can be seen. Like the model for the parallelogram this is made up of a stack of rectangles – but the width of each rectangle is slightly less than the width of the one below. Since they are all slightly different shapes it is easier to make this model with a thicker material than card. Expanded polystyrene ceiling tiles are suitable: they are easy to cut to size, and are thin enough to give a clear outline to the trapezium in the model.

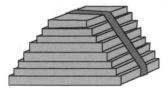

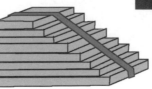

The model shows how any trapezium can be sheared into a right-angled trapezium, whose area can be partitioned into a rectangle and a triangle.

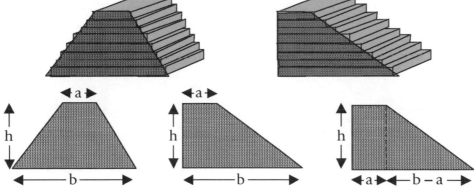

The area of the rectangle is $a \times h$, and the area of the triangle is $\frac{1}{2}(b - a) \times h$, so the total area of the trapezium is the sum of these, $a \times h + \frac{1}{2}(b - a) \times h$. This is not the standard formula for the area of a trapezium ($\frac{1}{2}(b + a) \times h$), but it is algebraically equivalent so the outcome is the same. The model makes sense in a way that the formula may not, so it can be recalled as a 'picture in the mind' and used to work out the formula when this is needed.

Shape, Space and Measures – Key Points

■ 'Mathematical' vocabulary may present a greater hurdle to some pupils than any aspect of the mathematics itself. It should be de-mystified as much as possible.

■ Meaningful movements, such as those used in signing, may help pupils to recall some mathematical terms.

■ **Area** and **perimeter** are often confused.

■ The distinction between area and perimeter can be established more firmly with the use of a different material to represent each measure.

■ Pupils who think more easily in pictures than in words and symbols struggle to remember formulas. A kinaesthetic and visual 'picture in the mind' is more meaningful, and therefore more memorable.

CHAPTER 9

Angles and Circles

- *Angle is a measure of turn. π is a ratio.*

- *These key concepts are often lost in static images on the printed page.*

- *Here again, pupils need visual and kinaesthetic 'pictures in the mind' that they can use as a basis for their mathematical thinking.*

a) Angle

An angle is a measure of turn. It is a *measure*, not a shape. Yet it is not classified as part of the Measures curriculum. It is commonly introduced, first and foremost, as a property of two-dimensional shapes.

So – what is an angle? Can we draw an angle, and print the drawing on the page?

Well … no. We can't. An angle is a measure of *turn*. A turn is a movement. And we cannot draw a movement. At best, we can draw a representation of the movement – something like this, perhaps:

But very often, right from the start, we speak and write of an angle, and represent it, as if it were a relationship between a pair of lines. The crucial arrow, to show that the curved line represents a movement, is lost:

And in the case of a right angle, convention has done away with even the hint of movement conveyed by the arc:

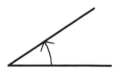

So here again, the predominance of print over objects and models in the representation of a mathematical concept may undermine pupils' understanding, and lead them to perceive an angle as a pair of straight lines rather than as a measure of turn. The kinaesthetic concept, which is all about movement, has been superseded by a static representation that is easier to print, but does nothing to convey the real meaning of angle.

Introducing angle with Shape rather than with Measures may lead to a common misconception about the relative sizes of angles.

These two lines:

are longer than these two lines:

so pupils may not unreasonably assume that this angle:

is greater than this angle:

They focus on the static, printed image of a pair of intersecting lines, rather than on the movement. The meaning of angle as a measure of turn, going from one direction to another, is lost.

In the Classroom – *Following Routes*

Pupils can follow a series of instructions involving movement forward (and backwards) a number of steps, and clockwise or anti-clockwise turns. The turns may be expressed first as simple fractions of a turn – quarter, half and three quarter turns, and then perhaps eighths of a turn. Later, pupils may use an angle machine (see below) to help them to turn through other fractions of a turn, or angles. Logo may be used to program a robot or a screen turtle to follow a path.

Activities (*activities* – not written exercises) that involve pupils in turning either themselves or an object are essential to establish a foundation for the understanding of angle as a measure of turn. An angle machine, cut from card, provides a good model of angle as a measure of a turning movement (see Photocopiable Resource Sheet 10). This can be marked off first in simple fractions of a turn – halves, quarters, thirds, sixths and, perhaps, eighths or twelfths. Degrees can be introduced later as just another, smaller, fraction of a turn.

In the Classroom – *Growing Angles*

The angle machine can be used to show an angle increasing steadily in size. As it passes through 90° it goes from being *acute* to being *obtuse*. Similarly, the idea of an 'angle' of 180°, which marks the barrier between *obtuse* and *reflex* angles, is much easier to grasp in the context of angle as a measure of turn. (The 'mathematical' terms *acute*, *obtuse* and *reflex* are Latin, not Greek this time – they just mean 'sharp', 'blunt' and 'reflected'.)

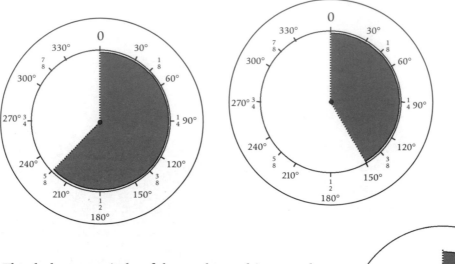

The dark centre-circle of the angle machine may be inserted on the plain side of the frame. This allows the teacher to show an angle 'growing' to a given size, which pupils can estimate.

If angle is thoroughly understood as a measure of turn then, here again, links may be made with other topics in different areas of the curriculum. A degree is just one particular example of a fraction of a turn. Degrees have been adopted by convention as the common units for the measure of angle, but they are not essentially different to other fractions of a turn. An analogue clock and a compass both rely on our ability to measure turn, although they use different units of measurement. On an analogue clock the hours, minutes and seconds are represented by the movement of the hands through twelfths and sixtieths of a whole turn, while a compass movement from, say, North to North East is an eighth of a turn. Linking angles firmly to the concept of fractions of a turn will help pupils to understand both, and to use them in a range of contexts.

In the ~~Classroom~~ Playground – *360° Protractor and Compass*

A giant 360° protractor marked out at 10° or 30° intervals in the playground will encourage pupils to think about angle as a measure of turn. Pupils can stand in the middle, then turn themselves through a given angle. This kinaesthetic experience will be much more meaningful, and memorable, than measuring or 'drawing' static angles on paper.

If the protractor is oriented so that '0' is to the north, and the points of the compass are added, then the link between angle as a measure of turn and compass directions will become clearer.

In the Classroom – *360 Degrees*

Pupils may be asked to find out *why* there are 360 degrees in a whole turn. Research into the history of mathematics should turn up the link to the Babylonians (for example, visit www.bbc.co.uk and search for '360 degrees') – but the pragmatic reasons for choosing 360, as opposed to any other number, may also be discussed. 360 has a lot of factors, including 3, 4, 5 and 6, so the external and internal angles of an equilateral triangle, a square, and a regular pentagon and hexagon are all a whole number of degrees. Pupils might like to consider what the effect would be of adopting a different convention – with, say, 100 degrees in a whole turn.

b) Angle Properties

If an angle is understood as a measure of turn, not as a static relationship between two straight lines, then many of its properties become easier to understand. For example, turning through a pair of angles on a line involves turning through a half turn, or 180°. So angles on a line, or *complementary* angles, have a total measure of 180°.

Opposite, corresponding and *alternate* angles (more hard word for easy ideas!) form an interconnected whole when they are placed in a grid of parallel lines. If the grid is squeezed, then all the angles change together.

A pair of opposite angles are, of course, opposite each other – so if one gets bigger, then so does the other. Similarly, a pair of alternate angles (the angles inside a Z-shape) will change together. Corresponding angles sit on a pair of parallel lines. The lines move together in the grid, so these angles, too, change together. The visual and kinaesthetic 'picture in the mind' is of the grid being squeezed, first one way and then the other. There are only two sets of angles, and all the angles in each set are the same size. They all change together when the grid is transformed.

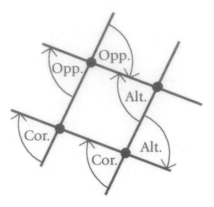

In the Classroom – *Angles in a Grid*

Pupils can make a grid of plastic or card strips, joined together with split pin paper fasteners. As the model is expanded and contracted the pairs of opposite, corrresponding and alternate angles increase or decrease together, always maintaining their equal measures.

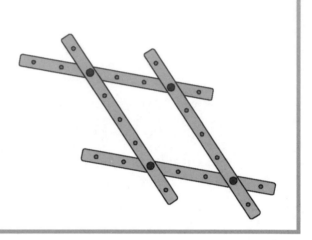

---

c) Circles and π

The formulas for the circumference and the area of a circle are probably the most consistently confused in the mathematics curriculum. There are few combinations of '2', 'r', 'π', 'r^2' and 'π^2' that do not turn up, at one time or another, masquerading as 'formulas' in the piles of exercise books from pupils who are struggling with the dimensions of a circle.

The first problem is π. What is it? Is it a number? Is it 3.14159 … , or whatever?

Well – not exactly. It is a ratio. π is the number of times I would have to walk across a circle in order to go the same distance as someone walking all the way round it.

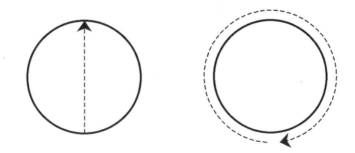

How many times *straight across* is the same as *all the way round*?

Using this kinaesthetic, movement-based approach, it is not hard to see that the number of times must be greater than 2. 2 would take me straight across and straight back, with no allowance made for the curved nature of the path around the edge of the circle.

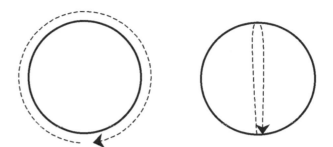

All the way round is more than *there and back*.
So π is more than 2.

But it cannot be as much as 4, because 4 times the distance straight across the middle of the circle would take me along the edge of a square which surrounds the circle. I would be walking further than the person going right round the edge of the circle, because she would be cutting the corners of my square.

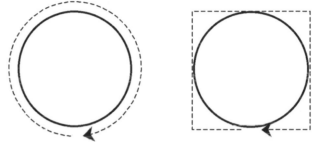

Round the circle is less than *round the square*.
So π is less than 4.

So π must be more than 2 but less than 4. As a first approximation, π is 3.

In fact, π is just a little bit more than 3. We can see this by thinking about a regular hexagon, made up of equilateral triangles.

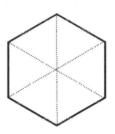

Walking right round the hexagon would take me along six triangle edge-lengths. This is exactly 3 times the distance straight across the middle.

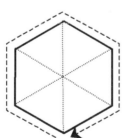

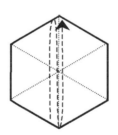

The distance *right round the hexagon*   is exactly   3 times the distance *straight across the middle*

A circle that just fits around the hexagon will have the same distance straight across the middle as the hexagon.

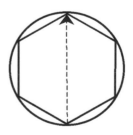

But the distance round the circle is a little bit more than the distance round the hexagon. So it is a little bit more than 3 times the distance straight across the middle. So π is a little bit more than 3.

π relates the distance all the way round a circle to the distance straight across it. It relates the *circumference* to the *diameter*, to use the popular (among mathematicians) jargon. The circumference is a little bit more than 3 times the diameter. This number, 'a little more than 3', is π. So the circumference is π times the diameter.

But that can create another confusion. π is defined in terms of the circumference and the *diameter* – the distance around the circle, and the distance *all* the way across. But the standard formulas for the circumference and area of a circle, $C = 2\pi r$, and $A = \pi r^2$, are expressed in terms of the circumference and the *radius*. This is the distance *half* way across the circle, not *all* the way. Pupils need to understand clearly the difference between these two distances – which is easy if they are part of a picture, on paper or in the mind, but much more difficult if they are just squiggles on the page.

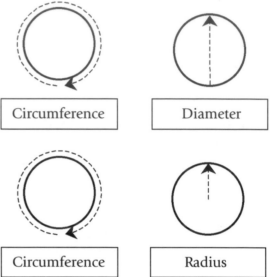

So we can see – literally *see* if we draw or imagine a circle that just fits around a regular hexagon – that the circumference of a circle is 3 and a bit, or π, times the diameter. This is the same as twice π times the radius, so $C = 2\pi r$. The formula can be taken directly out of the 'picture in the mind': there is no need to memorise it.

In the Classroom – *Circle Vocabulary*

'Mathematical' terms may be associated with movement to make them more memorable. For example, to learn the words associated with a circle, the pupil stands and chants:

I am the centre of the circle;

Radius; [Flings one arm straight out.]

Diameter; [Flings out the other arm.]

Circumference! [Turns right round on the spot.]

If some pupils are unwilling to take part in this activity, they will still benefit from watching other pupils (or the teacher) do it.

---

d) The Area of a Circle

A different 'picture in the mind' is needed to find the area of a circle. For this we can imagine a circle that is sliced from the top to the centre, and then opened out into a wide, low triangle.

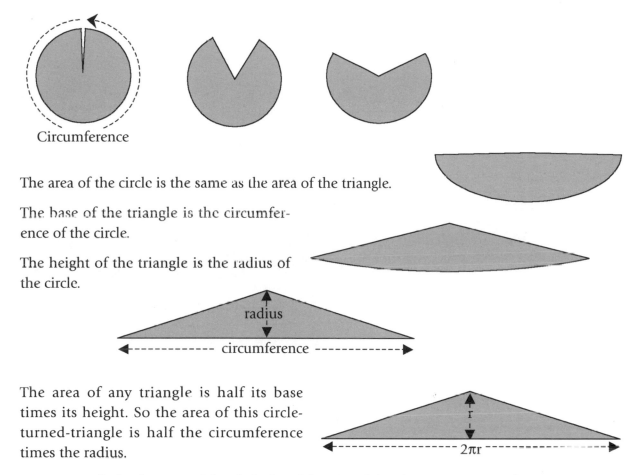

Circumference

The area of the circle is the same as the area of the triangle.

The base of the triangle is the circumference of the circle.

The height of the triangle is the radius of the circle.

The area of any triangle is half its base times its height. So the area of this circle-turned-triangle is half the circumference times the radius.

In symbols, the area of the circle (*or* of the triangle) is $\frac{1}{2} \times 2\pi r \times r$, or πr^2.

Here again, the aim of the models and images is to establish visual and kinaesthetic 'pictures in the mind' that pupils can recall later. These will enable the pupils not to *remember* the formulas but, rather, to *re-construct* them when they are needed.

In the Classroom – *Area of a circle*

A model may be made, consisting of a series of rings of beads that can be opened out to form a triangle.

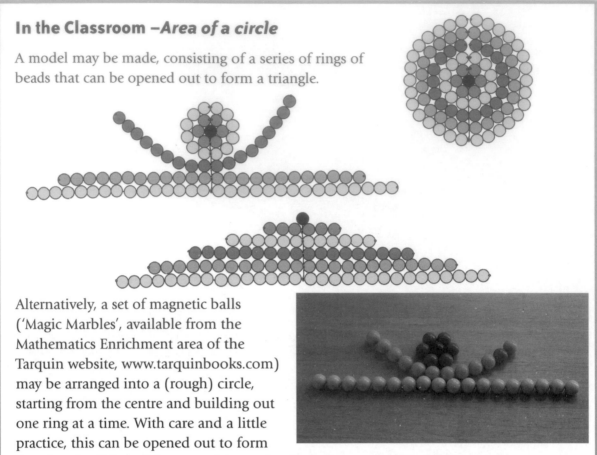

Alternatively, a set of magnetic balls ('Magic Marbles', available from the Mathematics Enrichment area of the Tarquin website, www.tarquinbooks.com) may be arranged into a (rough) circle, starting from the centre and building out one ring at a time. With care and a little practice, this can be opened out to form the triangle. Either of these models can be shown on an overhead projector.

Angles and Circles – Key Points

- An angle is a measure of **turn**, not a pair of static straight lines.

- Activities that involve pupils moving an object or themselves through angles will help them to recognise angle as a measure of turn.

- A degree is just one particular fraction of a turn.

- Other fractions of a turn are used to measure time on an analogue clock, or movement between the points of a compass.

- **Opposite, corresponding** and **alternate** angles are pairs of angles that change together on a transforming grid.

- π is the number of times I would have to walk straight across a circle (the **diameter**) in order to go the same distance as someone walking all the way round it (the **circumference**).

- π is a bit more than 3, so the circumference of a circle is a bit more than 3 times the diameter.

- A circle may be opened out into a triangle whose base is the circumference, and whose height is the radius. The area of the triangle (half its base times its height) is the same as the area of the circle (half its circumference times its radius).

- The formulas for the circumference and area of a circle can be taken directly out of the models and the 'pictures in the mind'. They do not need to be memorised.

CHAPTER 10

Data Handling

- *Data Handling lends itself to a more practical approach than other parts of the mathematics curriculum.*

- *Pupils are likely to engage with activities in which they collect, process and represent their own data.*

- *Some pupils' confidence may be undermined by the sheer quantity of numerical data in lists and tables.*

- *Graphical representations can convey the overall shape of the data, but they may disguise unreliably small sample sizes.*

- *Some data-handling activities can involve shapes rather than numerical data.*

a) Seeing the Data

Data handling has a rather special place in the school mathematics curriculum. It is generally agreed that an understanding of statistics and their representation is essential in a literate and numerate society, if only to help us to distinguish the 'damn lies' from the 'statistics' in political speeches or newspaper articles. But data handling is a relative newcomer to the school curriculum, and this may be why it is often approached in a different way to the rest of mathematics. Statistics, after all, have to be about something – and that 'something' may affect the way the subject is presented and discussed. It may provide a context for the lists and tables of figures, and this can help to give them some meaning. Mathematics textbook writers and examiners are often happy enough to require pupils to do a calculation, or to find a length or an angle in an abstract diagram, with no context. But if pupils are asked to draw a bar chart or to find the mean of a set of figures, then this must be in order to represent and process some data – and that data is likely to have a context. It may even relate to observations or results that the pupils themselves have collected. Generally speaking, school mathematics exercises in data handling are more likely than those in other areas of the curriculum to be in context.

The raw data itself – the lists of figures and tables – can be quite daunting. But many school data-handling activities involve data that is summarised and represented in a range of graphical forms, and this can make the topic more meaningful to pupils who think more easily in pictures than in numbers and symbols. For example, the same information about a group of pupils who go to dance and to music lessons might be shown in two forms – in a table and in a Venn diagram.

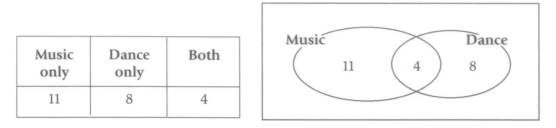

Music only	Dance only	Both
11	8	4

The diagram brings out the relationships between the figures in a way that the simple table cannot do. The total group of dancers, for example, is shown in the right-hand loop, while the dancers who also go to music lessons are shown in the middle where the two loops overlap. The position of the figures on the diagram mirrors the positions of the pupils they represent in the two groups.

A long list of figures may convey little in itself, while a simple bar chart gives the numbers a dimension that makes it possible to take in the overall shape of the data at a glance. For example, the table below shows the number of goals scored by a team in each of twelve matches one season.

Match	1st	2nd	3rd	4th	5th	6th	7th	8th	9th	10th	11th	12th
Goals	2	0	3	2	3	2	2	0	4	1	3	2

This raw data can be collected into a frequency table, to show how often the team scored 0, 1, 2, 3 or 4 goals.

Number of goals	0	1	2	3	4
Number of matches	2	1	5	3	1

But this table still presents a bewildering array of figures. The same information can be presented more graphically in a bar chart.

The bar chart gives an overall picture of the data. For example, it enables us to see at once, with no need for any computation, that in more than half of the matches the team scored two or three goals. Graphical representations like these can help pupils to get beyond the detail of the specific figures to look at their overall

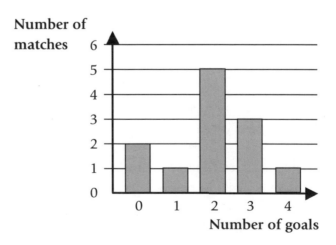

shape, and the relationships between the different parts. This will enable them to grasp the whole pattern without being distracted, and possibly confused, by the individual values that make up the total data set.

In the Classroom – *Scattered Pupils*

The pupils themselves can provide a useful starting point for a lot of work with data handling. For example, each point on a scatter graph can represent a pupil, so the meaning of the statistics and their representation will be clear and relevant.

Prepare a large grid with the axes labelled with the two measures whose relationship is to be graphed. For instance, the scatter graph might show two body measurements, such as *height* and *hand span*, or it might show *distance travelled to school* against *time taken*.

Each pupil takes a sticky label, such as a small Post-it note, writes their initials on the label, and sticks it in the correct position on the scatter graph. If this is done bit by bit, with different groups of pupils adding their labels one after another, the overall pattern of the relationship between the two sets of data will emerge gradually. Each pupil's identity with one particular point on the scatter graph – 'That label there is *me!*' – will help them to understand the whole diagram as a collection of individual data points, without losing sight of the overall shape of the data. With this approach there are no lists of figures to be processed. Rather, the graph is built up directly from the data.

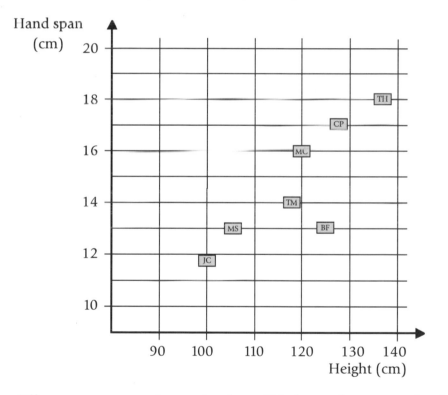

Plotting different measures against each other will help pupils to recognise the concepts of strong, weak and no correlation. Either of the graphs described above, for example, is likely to produce some degree of positive correlation – taller pupils are more likely to have a larger hand span than shorter, and pupils who travel further are likely to take longer. On the other hand, *hand span* is not likely to correlate with *distance travelled to school*, and a plotting of these two factors may show the lack of relationship clearly.

Once they have grasped the concept of a scatter graph, the pupils themselves may suggest other data sets that can be graphed against one another.

b) Using Non-numerical Data

Many data-handling activities require pupils to work with a lot of numbers. Data sets are often composed solely of numbers, sometimes in large collections. For those pupils who think more easily in pictures and movements, the numbers may get in the way of their understanding of key concepts of data handling.

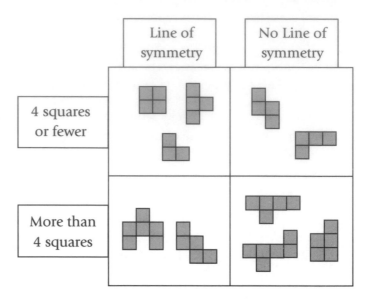

But some aspects of the topic can be introduced with shapes, and this may offer a more effective way in for pupils for whom numbers will always remain suspect and hard to grasp. In Chapter 8, *Shape, Space and Measures*, we saw how shapes made with squares joined together may be placed on a scatter graph according to their areas and perimeters. Similarly, different kinds of sorting diagrams, such as Carroll or Venn diagrams, may be introduced using a set of shapes. Activities like these, which bypass the numbers and enable pupils to build up a graph or a diagram directly as the data is collected, will help them to understand the principles of data handling without having to worry about the figures.

In the Classroom – *Sorting Pupils*

The pupils themselves may again provide a good entry point for work on sorting diagrams. Pupils may be physically arranged on a giant sorting diagram marked out on the floor, with the cells labelled with two different pairs of mutually exclusive criteria – for example, *Girls* and *Boys*, and *Left-handed* and *Right-handed*.

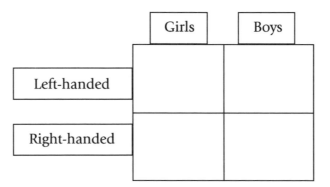

This sort, or a similar one on a Venn diagram, may again be recorded on paper using a sticky label to represent each pupil.

---

c) Mean and Median

As well as collecting and representing data, pupils may need to process it, for example by finding the mean of a set of numbers. The definition of the mean, and the procedures to be followed to work it out, are usually presented entirely in symbols, without any pictures or models. So here again, as in so many areas of mathematics, there is a danger that the rules will be learnt by rote, with little understanding – and then forgotten.

But the mean of a set of numbers is a very simple idea. It is the answer to the question, *What would it be if I shared them all out equally?* This can be demonstrated effectively with a set of sticks of interlocking cubes, representing the numbers whose mean is to be found. For example, to find the mean of five numbers, 7, 4, 8, 2 and 9, five sticks may be made:

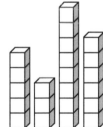

The cubes in the sticks can then be rearranged to even them out, giving five sticks of 6 cubes – so the mean of the five numbers is 6.

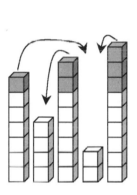

In this case the mean is a whole number – but it clearly need not be. For example, take the mean of 5, 3, 8 and 6.

Most of the cubes can be shared out equally, to give four sticks of 5 cubes each.

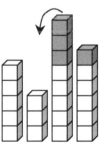

But two cubes will be left over.

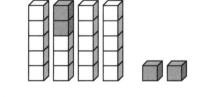

These last 2 cubes must also be shared out. There are 2 cubes to share between four sticks, or an extra half cube for each stick, giving a mean of 5½.

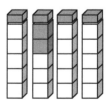

This model helps to explain why the mean of a set of whole numbers may not be a whole number.

Rearranging the sticks in order of height will help pupils to see the value of the median – the middle value.

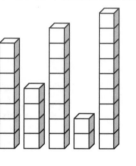
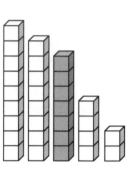

In the set of five sticks, the third, which has a height of 7, is in the middle, so the median of this set of numbers is 7.

When we have an even number of sticks, however, there is no stick in the middle – so the median must lie halfway between the two middle sticks.

These are 6 and 5 cubes high, so the median of these four numbers is 5½.

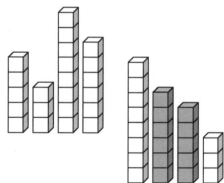

d) Sample Sizes

Some pupils who have difficulty working with graphical representations, and who need numbers to give the data meaning, may be puzzled by statistical diagrams that do not include figures. On the other hand, visual and kinaesthetic thinkers are more likely to be able to draw conclusions from the overall shape of the data, rather than from the detailed figures. For example, the pie charts on the next page show the proportions of boys and girls, and the proportions of right and left-handed pupils, in one group.

From these pie charts it is possible to tell, for instance, that all the boys could be right-handed, but not all the right-handed pupils are boys. But we cannot tell how many boys, or how

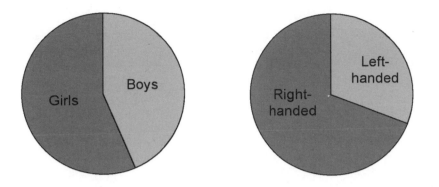

many right-handed pupils, there are in the group. The pie charts could represent a group of any size – a single class, a school, all the pupils in the country, or even all the pupils in the world.

When we are not told how large the group is, however, there is a danger that conclusions may be drawn on the basis of too small a sample. A similar problem may arise when data is presented in percentages. Percentages are convenient because they can be used to compare proportions easily – it is difficult to tell immediately whether 132 out of 360 is more or less than 13 out of 30, but it is obvious that $36\frac{2}{3}$%. is less than $43\frac{1}{3}$%. But because percentages are always out of a hundred, they can convey a totally false impression that there are at least a hundred members in the sample. For example, it is arithmetically correct to say that 3 out of 4 is 75%. But in a statistical context this may not be useful. If three out of a group of four pupils can ride a bicycle then all we can really say is that those three pupils can, and that one pupil cannot, ride. To talk about 'seventy-five per cent' of the pupils being able to ride gives a spurious generality to the observation.

The idea that samples need to be big enough to be confident that the results are valid is not easy to grasp. One approach is to find ways to deliberately 'cook' a set of data, by choosing only the left-handed girls and the right-handed boys, for instance, and then seeing what conclusions might be falsely drawn.

Data Handling – Key Points

■ Data-handling exercises are more likely to involve contextualised problems than those in other areas of mathematics.

■ Pupils may engage more effectively with activities which involve processing and representing data that they have collected themselves.

■ Large quantities of numerical data may undermine the confidence of visual and kinaesthetic learners, but its representation in graphical form makes it more comprehensible.

■ Graphical representations of data can help pupils to get beyond the detail of the specific figures to look at their overall shape, and the relationships between the different parts.

■ Some aspects of data handling may be introduced using shapes rather than numbers. This may make the underlying concepts more accessible to some pupils.

■ The process of finding the mean and median of a set of data may be represented with a model made of interlocking cubes.

■ Both graphical representations, such as pie charts, and data that is presented as percentages may disguise unreliably small sample sizes.

CONCLUSIONS

This book is about teaching mathematics to pupils with learning *differences*. These are the pupils who favour a visual and kinaesthetic, rather than an auditory, thinking style, and for whom the conventional print-based curriculum may not be appropriate. Their learning differences may, on occasion, lead to learning *difficulties*, but such difficulties are an outcome of inappropriate teaching. They are not, in themselves, a cause of failure.

Visual and kinaesthetic thinkers are likely to benefit from an approach that focuses on the development of models and images that make key mathematical concepts manifest. The ideas and activities described in this book offer examples of this approach, and are designed to help pupils to understand, not just the *how*, but also, crucially, the *why* of mathematics. Teachers may draw on these suggestions to develop materials that will support their own pupils' understanding.

It is still not clear, however, how many of our pupils might benefit from the approach suggested here, or how much difference it could make. Nor do we know where these pupils are – whether they are distributed evenly throughout the educational system, or are more likely to be found in particular types of school or institution. There is some evidence that many dyslexic pupils can learn to read more easily using a visual and kinaesthetic approach, rather than the more conventional decoding of printed symbols, although, as Kay and Yeo explain, different dyslexic pupils have different thinking styles. (Davis, 1994; Kay and Yeo, 2003). Pupils with Down's syndrome often show 'strengths for visual learning' (Bird and Buckley, 2004), and they may benefit from visual and kinaesthetic materials at an appropriate level. There is anecdotal evidence that a disproportionate number of youngsters in Pupil Referral Units, and in special schools for emotionally and behaviourally disturbed children, are strong spatial thinkers. And even if they manage to remain in mainstream education, the print-based assessment system may place visual and kinaesthetic learners in the 'bottom set' for mathematics, and make it difficult for them to show what they understand in formal written tests. But there has not yet been a thorough study to establish the proportion of pupils in different settings who have different preferred learning styles. This is an area of research that could prove rewarding.

Of course, nobody uses only one thinking style. The great majority of pupils in most classrooms do access much of the curriculum more or less effectively through the conventional auditory channels. But an approach that focuses on the use of 'models to think with' to develop pupils' understanding of mathematics is likely to help all the pupils in the group. We all know that *If it's good for special, then it's good for mainstream*. But even more significant here is the inverse: *If it's bad for mainstream, then it's bad for special*. Teaching that relies on the pupils' acquisition of meaningless algorithms will serve the highest achievers poorly – but for those in the 'bottom set' it can be a disaster.

As they stand, the philosophy, ideas and materials in this book are just yet more print. If they are to serve any purpose at all then they have to be activated. And that is down to teachers teaching mathematics – in classrooms, in units, at home, wherever they may be. Learning differences are not a weakness to be remedied; they are a strength to be exploited. They are not a difficulty to be overcome; they are an opportunity to be seized. They are not a failure to be regretted; they are a success to be celebrated.

Let's do it!

References

1. Introduction

Mike Askew et al., 1997: *Effective Teachers of Numeracy*. London: King's College.
Paul Black and Dylan Wiliam, 1998: *Inside the Black Box*. London: King's College.
Steve Chinn, 2004: *The Trouble with Maths*. London: Routledge Falmer.
Tandi Clausen-May, 2001: *An Approach to Test Development*. London: NFER-Nelson.
Keith Devlin, 2000: *The Maths Gene*. London: Weidenfeld and Nicolson.
NFER-Nelson, 2001: *Cognitive Abilities Test*. London: NFER-Nelson.
Pauline Smith and Tom Lord, 2002: *Spatial Reasoning Tests*. London: NFER-Nelson.
Steve Strand, 2003: *Getting the Best from CAT*. London: NFER-Nelson.

2. The Concept of Number

Brian Butterworth, 1999: *The Mathematical Brain*. London: Macmillan
Eva Grauberg, 1998: *Elementary Mathematics and Language Difficulties*. London: Whurr Publishers.

3. Models for Multiplication and Division

Steve Chinn, 1998: *Sum Hope: Breaking the Numbers Barrier*. London: Souvenir Press.
QCA, 2000: *Standards at Key Stage 3 – Mathematics. Report on the 1999 national curriculum assessments for 14-year-olds*. London: QCA.

5. Fractions

Tandi Clausen-May and Hanna Vappula, 2005: 'Context in maths test questions – Does it make a difference?' Paper presented to the British Congress for Mathematics Education, Warwick 2005.
Tandi Clausen-May, Graham Ruddock and Hanna Vappula, 2005: *Progress in Maths 4–14*. London: NFER-Nelson.

7. Algebra

Geoff Giles, 1994: *Algebra Through Geometry*. Stirling: DIME Projects.

8. Shape, Space and Measures

Tandi Clausen-May, 2003: *Mathematical Minds – A Guide to Assessing Attainment Target One*. London: NFER-Nelson.

Conclusions

G. Bird and S.J. Buckley, 2004: 'Number skills for individuals with Down syndrome – An overview'. The Down Syndrome Information Network. http://www.downsyndrome.net/library/dsii/09/01/.

Ronald Davis, 1994: *The Gift of Dyslexia*. London: Souvenir Press.

Julie Kay and Dorian Yeo, 2003: *Dyslexia and Maths*. London: David Fulton.

PHOTOCOPIABLE RESOURCE SHEETS

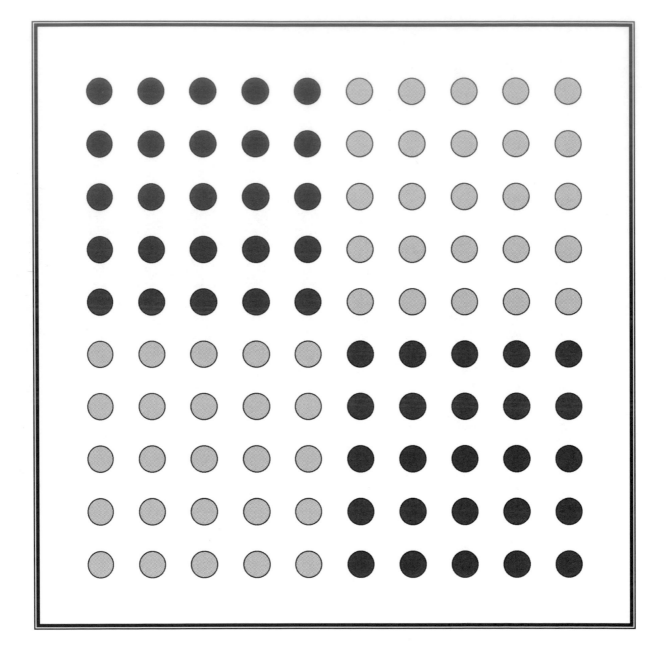

Slavonic Abacus – OHP Grid

Teaching Maths to Pupils with Different Learning Styles, © Tandi Clausen-May, 2005, Chapter 2, Resource Sheet 1
Copy onto an Overhead Transparency sheet.

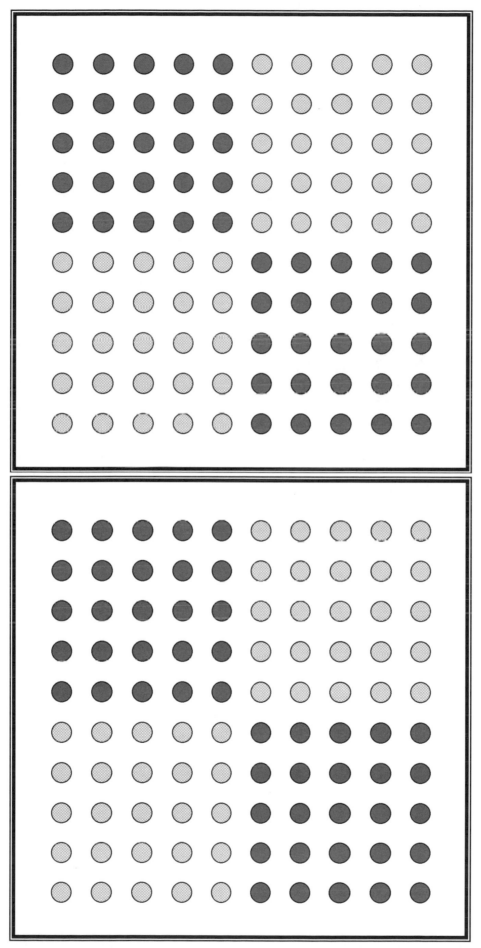

Slavonic Abacus – Pupils' Grids

Teaching Maths to Pupils with Different Learning Styles, © Tandi Clausen-May, 2005, Chapter 2, Resource Sheet 2
Copy onto card, and cut out.

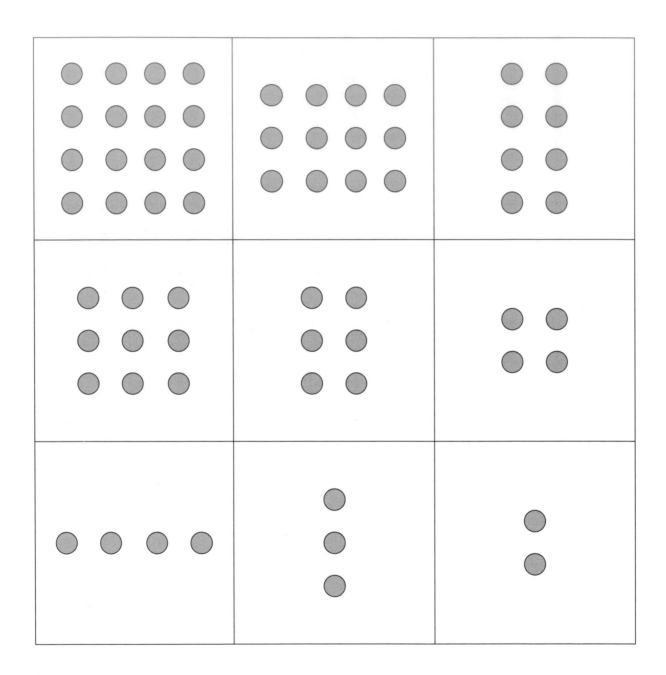

Spatial Multiplication Array Cards

Teaching Maths to Pupils with Different Learning Styles, © Tandi Clausen-May, 2005, Chapter 3,
Resource Sheet 3
Copy onto card, and cut out.

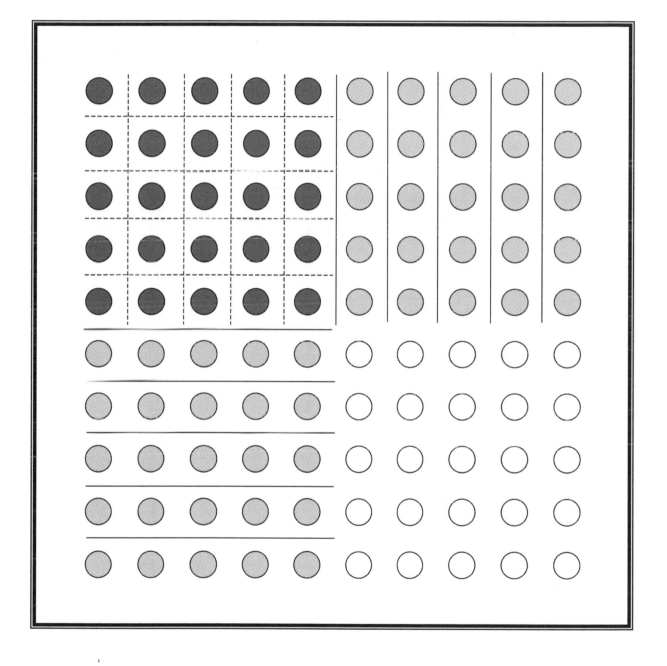

Slavonic Abacus – OHP Multiplication Grid

Teaching Maths to Pupils with Different Learning Styles, © Tandi Clausen-May, 2005, Chapter 3, Resource Sheet 4

Copy onto an Overhead Transparency sheet.

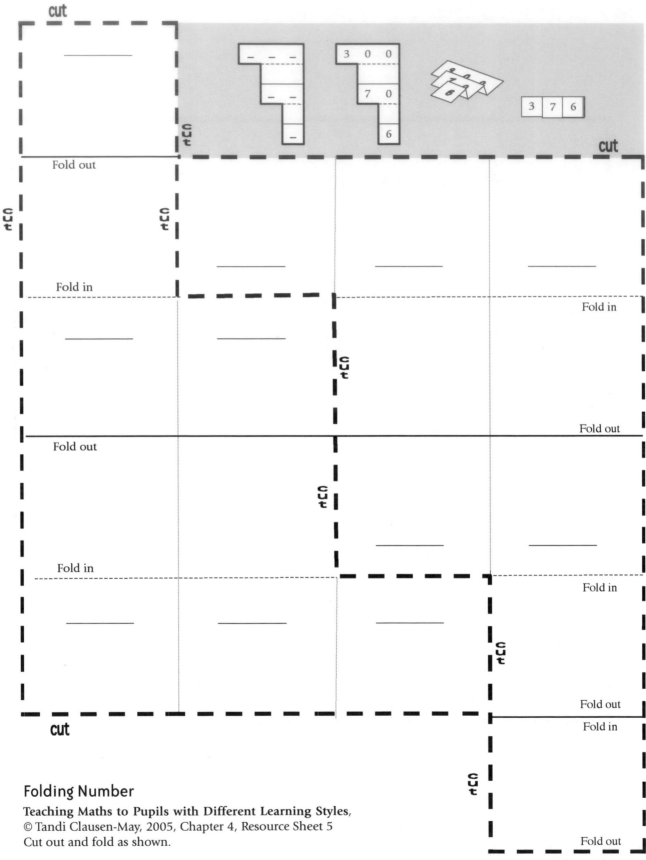

Folding Number

Fold out

- -

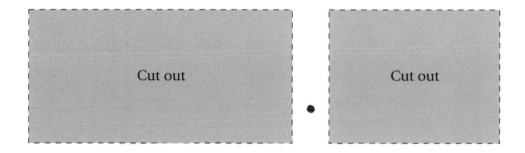

Cut out   Cut out

•

- -

Fold out

Decimal Slide – Holder

Teaching Maths to Pupils with Different Learning Styles, © Tandi Clausen-May, 2005, Chapter 4, Resource Sheet 6
Cut out windows. Fold along dotted lines. Insert Decimal Slide Number (see Resource Sheet 7).

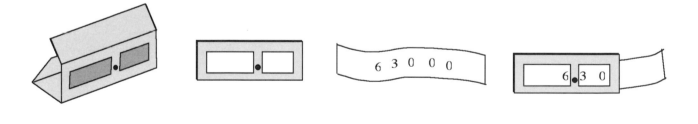

- -

Fold out

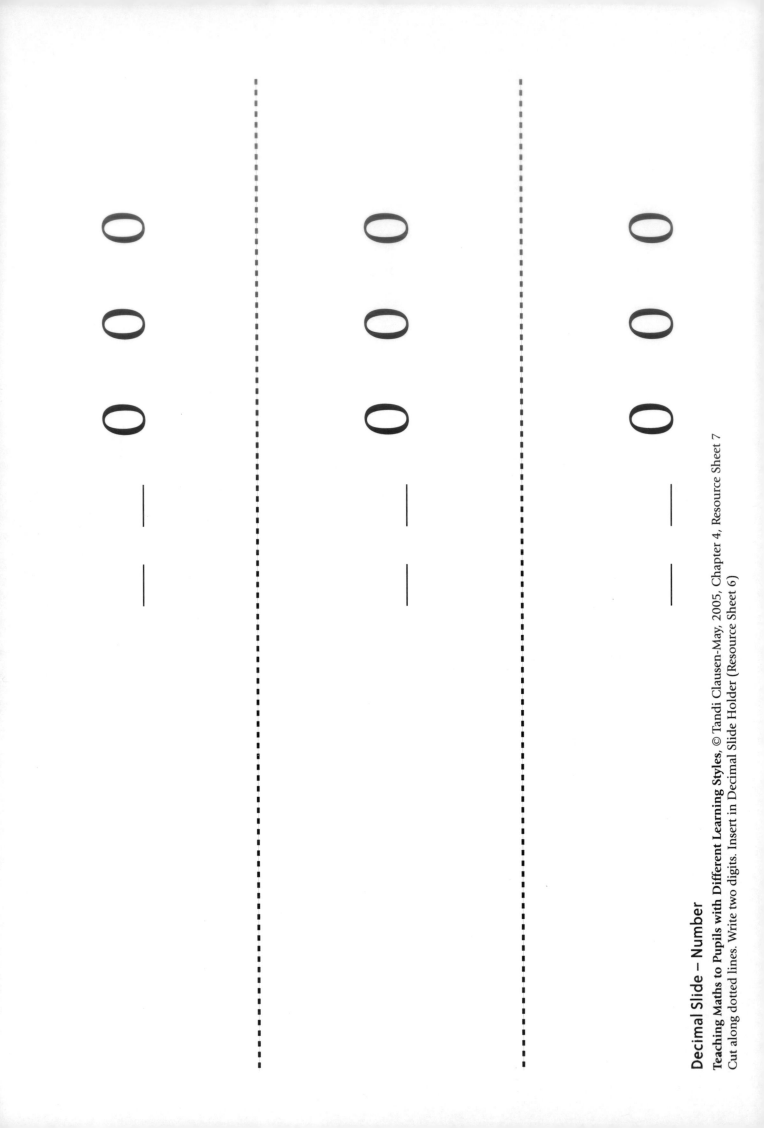

Decimal Slide – Number

Teaching Maths to Pupils with Different Learning Styles, © Tandi Clausen-May, 2005, Chapter 4, Resource Sheet 7

Cut along dotted lines. Write two digits. Insert in Decimal Slide Holder (Resource Sheet 6)

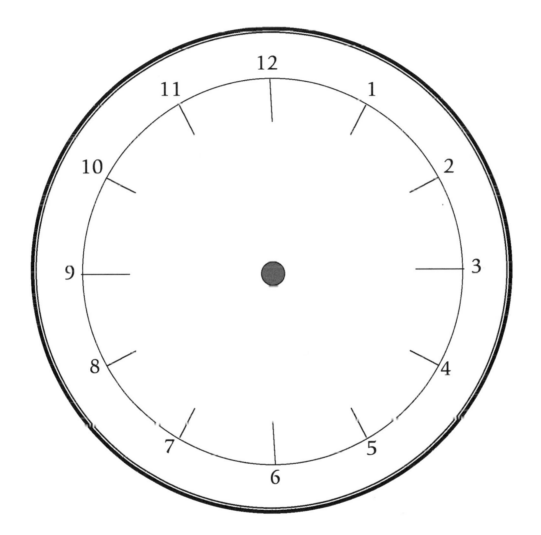

OHP Fraction Clock

Teaching Maths to Pupils with Different Learning Styles, © Tandi Clausen-May, 2005, Chapter 5, Resource Sheet 8
Copy onto an Overhead Transparency sheet.
Cut out a 'pointer' from card, and attach it with a split pin fastener.

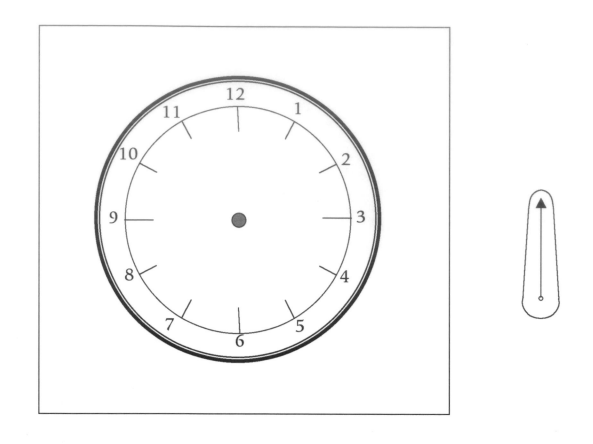

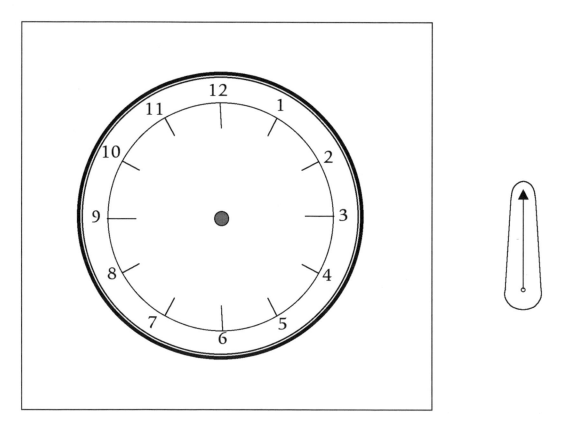

Pupils' Fraction Clocks

Teaching Maths to Pupils with Different Learning Styles, © Tandi Clausen-May, 2005, Chapter 5, Resource Sheet 9
Copy onto card, and cut out. Attach the 'pointer' with a split pin fastener.

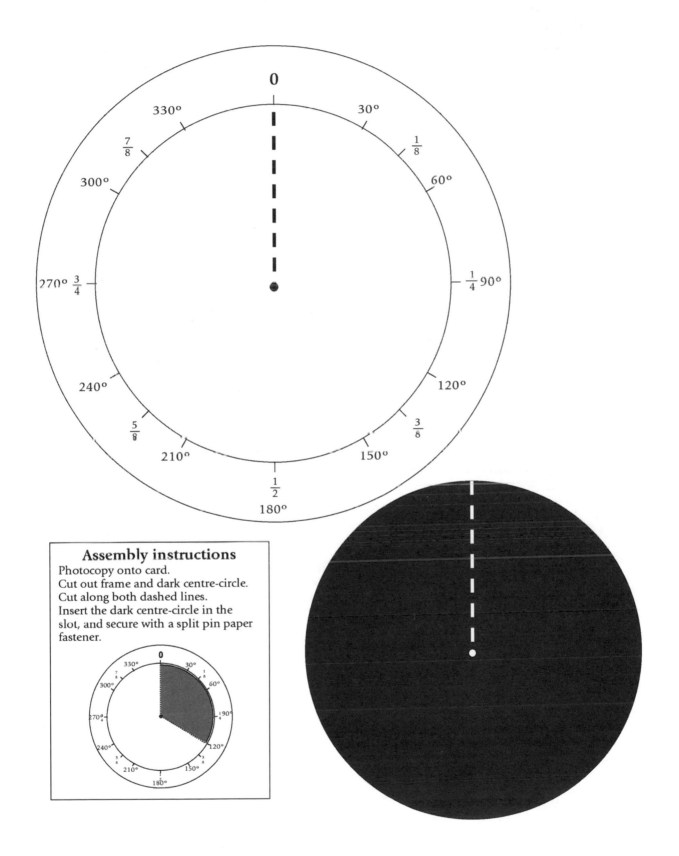

Angle Machine

Teaching Maths to Pupils with Different Learning Styles, © Tandi Clausen-May, 2005, Chapter 9, Resource Sheet 10

INDEX

Entries in *italic* refer to activities.